Sounding Out Your Feelings

In the Gardens of Your Mind and Heart

Simple powerful self-explorations using your voice to enhance your feelings of well-being

Margaret Geard

Copyright © 2026 Margaret Geard. All Rights Reserved

No part of this book may be reproduced, stored in a retrieval system, or transmitted in any form or by any means—electronic, mechanical, photocopying, recording, or otherwise—without prior written permission from the author.

ISBN: 979-8-218-92021-0

For my mother, Hazel Cummins Nothrop,
an accomplished violinist
and my very first voice teacher

CONTENTS

Introduction 7

PART 1 9

    Sound is vibration, frequency, and resonance: It creates. . . . 12

    What is Sounding? 13

    Why this emphasis on self-care? 15

    How do I use my voice for Sounding? 16

    How does Sounding work? 23

    What is frequency? 25

    What is the reality you want to experience? 26

    How do you know if your intention is working? 28

    How do we access our feelings during Sounding? 29

    How do I get into Quiet-mind? 31

    A plan for Sounding Out Your Feelings sessions 33

PART 2 37

    EXPLORATION 1: Your Journey Begins 39

    EXPLORATION 2: The Keepers at the Gateway to Your Mind—and the filters through which you see the world and operate in it 45

    EXPLORATION 3: The Dragon of Illusion: How you see yourself through the eyes of others 57

    EXPLORATION 4: Resounding in the Corridors of Power . . 67

    EXPLORATION 5: In the Hall of Mirrors 75

    EXPLORATION 6: In the Land Where Every Wish is Granted: Mind what you think. 81

    EXPLORATION 7: Playing as the Children of Terra: Your natural impulses lead you where you intend to go 91

    EXPLORATION 8: If You Ruled the World: Loving what you do for a living. 99

PART 3 107

   Introduction: Sounding Out New Territory on the Way to Your Heart 109

   EXPLORATION 9: Happy? Me? I Guess I am, probably .. 115
   EXPLORATION 10: Abandoned? Left Out of the Picture?.. 123
   EXPLORATION 11: Heavenly Scent, or Not? 129
   EXPLORATION 12: The Pitter-Patter of Iron-Clad Boots.. 135
   EXPLORATION 13: Lucky Thirteen? 141
   EXPLORATION 14: Grace Comes in the Morning 145
   EXPLORATION 15: Happy Days 149
   EXPLORATION 16: Pets Passing–Waiting for them to go. . 155

PART 4 161

   EXPLORATION 17: Guardian Angels 167
   EXPLORATION 18: Earth Angels...................... 173
   EXPLORATION 19: Death Singing..................... 179
   EXPLORATION 20: Fear of the Body's Frailties 183
   EXPLORATION 21: "Oh, Death, where is Thy Sting?" (Handel, *The Messiah*) 187

PART 5 193

   EXPLORATION 22: What is Soul Growth? 197
   EXPLORATION 23: Valuing and Loving Who You Are ... 201
   EXPLORATION 24: Your Consciousness. What is it? 205
   EXPLORATION 25: Listening to Your Environment and How it Affects You 211
   EXPLORATION 26: Is it Time Now to Tap Your Emotional Reset Key? 215
   EXPLORATION 27: "Futurizing" 219
   EXPLORATION 28: Mother Earth Is Sharing Her Precious Jewels with Us. 225
   EXPLORATION 29: Do I Have a Real Purpose While Here on Earth?.. 231
   EXPLORATION 30: Wherever You Go, Here You Are.... 235

Acknowledgements.. 239

INTRODUCTION

I wrote this book, *Sounding Out Your Feelings,* for those of you who may feel the need of a new, effective tool for your self-care in these times of unpredictability—one that offers you new ways to use your own human voice to enhance your sense of overall well-being in body, mind, spirit, and heart. This is not a book about singing, nor is it about how to sing.

Perhaps you sometimes listen to your favorite music and feel so much the better for it. This is a lift for a short while, and a good one. However, using your own voice to target areas of the body or of the self, with intention and the skills you will gain as you work through this material, can produce effects that truly enhance your sense of wellbeing and make changes in your life.

In the following pages you will find some explanations of how Sounding works and an easy and simple way to use your voice for Sounding. Next, come a series of stand-alone Explorations offering ideas on how you may make changes in your life, to be more at ease with who you are. You will be guided, by my words, through each experience of Sounding Out Your Feelings. You will use an intention (that is, what you hope to have happen from the Exploration you have chosen to do), joined with the vibrations of your own vocal sounds, to bring about a new and different way to view your life.

For many years I have offered classes and workshops in this form of voice usage, Sounding, and I know from my students' stories, and personally, how effectively it works. I have come to realize just how much the feelings are involved when people made sounds together or on their own.

Have fun exploring the amazing self that you are as you travel these Explorations.

Margaret

PART 1

Explanations about Sounding Out Your Feelings

Before we begin this series of self-explorations into yourself and your inner self, there are some things you might want to know about Sounding and sound and self-care as I refer to them in this book.

Sounding is about you using your own human voice to bring about personal changes that may lead you to a more satisfying life. It is my intention to lead you to experience the vibrational sounds of your own voice as a tool for opening to an awareness of yourself. You must truly desire to change. This is serious work, not just an intellectual exercise in gaining information.

So, let us journey together through the Explorations and use them as keys that open the door for you to experience a greater sense of who you are.

The vibrational frequencies of your vocal sounds bypass your thinking self and go straight to the level of your cells, causing changes there. Think about how radiation therapy targets cancer cells to eliminate, or change, them. The vibrations of your vocal sounds target cells that are 'out of tune,' in a state of unwellness, causing those cells to vibrate at their optimal vibratory rate, to a state of wellness.

Why do we concentrate on the cells of your body during Sounding?

The body is your vehicle in this physical reality for housing your soul (or whatever you want to call it), that part of you that is largely unknown but which operates those parts of yourself that have been called the autonomic systems, and you—body, mind, heart—through to the cellular level. Your trillions of cells are powerhouses of energy and consciousness, vibrating, emitting minute sounds. When we use our voices in Sounding, we invoke these sounds to be in harmony with other sounds around them to bring you into a sense of well-being.

However, what we believe and think about life and ourselves helps the soul to operate our bodies also. But we have free will to make decisions for ourselves. The cells of our body respond to these, bringing about that sense of wellbeing—or not. So, we are working at the cellular level, sometimes called quantum healing, with the vibrations and frequencies of the sounds of your voice.

This process is intuitive. Your emotions are aroused by your sounds in Sounding before you recognize which or why. You will discover how to cope safely with these emotions. You are always in charge here, and you can stop any time. I stress here that we are doing self-care, not medical care. When the going gets rough, get help.

Sound is vibration, frequency, and resonance: It creates.

As we have safety rules and regulations around the use of electrical energy and atomic energy, we might also regard the power of sonic energy in a similar light. We have but a primitive knowledge of both electrical energy and atomic energy, yet we use them with incredible success. All the while we use restraint, careful in our usage of these powerful forces of nature. Remember, you are responsible for what you create with your vocal sounds. The use of intention and expectation are critical here, and we will explore this idea later in the book. For now, just know.

My dear fellow traveler, value this incredible gift of your human voice and use it wisely and well. Some people develop their voices for singing opera or songs, or in speaking for oratory purposes. Sounding Out Your Feelings gives you a real opportunity to make valuable use of your vibratory reverberations using Sounding for well-being. Also, you are giving your intentions a vibrational boost from these vocal sounds. In fact, Sounding is an attempt to match the same frequencies of your thoughts in purposeful intending. Powerful stuff!

What is Sounding?

In Sounding, you use your own human voice to enhance your sense of well-being by targeting the vibrational frequencies of your vocal sounds to out-of-tune cells, when you are not feeling well, for instance. Through the use of your intention, that which you desire to experience, you are expressing your feelings, some new, some perhaps long held deep inside yourself, and forgotten. Your body holds these for you, often in the form of tension, or muscular hardness, or a vague feeling of discomfort—in the hands, or neck, for instance—or of not feeling so well and of not being happy. With Sounding, the body can release feelings and tensions as you allow the feelings to come up again, but only as much as you can deal with, at the time, safely.

Sounding can also provide a way to access ideas, thoughts, or beliefs which may have been holding you back from moving on in your life to something new and more fulfilling.

Sounding can sometimes help you to identify thoughts that are running around in your conscious mind but are quite unnoticed by you in your self-talk. Making sounds from your body automatically, or intuitively, as we do in Sounding, may help you to loosen these thoughts so they 'float up' to a more obvious place in your thoughts. Here you may examine these thoughts and deal with them as you see fit. And, you can use Sounding—making sounds with your own vocal tones—with intention, to bypass the thinking self for a few moments to allow the more unobserved portions of yourself to speak to you.

Using Sounding in this way requires a different way of listening, of paying attention to yourself, the inner and outer you. All of this is done with your conscious permission. You are always in charge. You will know when you have done enough to throw light into the darkened corners of yourself, stimulating your being into action. You will know how far to go in a session for your comfort. The release of old energies can be exhilarating and refreshing.

Why this emphasis on self-care?

Self-care of the *body*—showering, brushing teeth, caring for the skin, etc.—is physical upkeep. Here, we are interested in the care of your feelings, emotions, thoughts, and beliefs—your inner life. With Sounding, you emphasize the parts of yourself that perhaps you tend to not think about, and which form the operating system of you as a person.

Let's now explore several vital elements of Sounding:

The Quiet-mind is when you turn off the outside world for a while. You go into a kind of daydream state. Quiet-mind allows you to drift off to a non-thought area of your mind. Or maybe you have your own meditation practice or prayerful state to use for these purposes. Quiet-mind is useful for Sounding in that here you are free to allow yourself to make the sounds that come unbidden. These are the vibrational frequencies needed to bring about the essence of your intention. Necessarily, you remain in this wonderful state after Sounding for a while to allow the penetration of the sounds made to do their work of your intention, what you want to experience in your reality. We call this the Silence. As you delve into this work, and it will be work in some ways, pleasure in other ways, you will find your own methods of accomplishing these elements - with a little help here and there from me, your guide and storyteller.

If you want to know the secrets of the Universe think: energy, vibration, and frequency.
—Nikola Tesla

How do I use my voice for Sounding?

Sounding uses a quiet singing tone, or sound, which is meditative in nature, not shouted or noisy, and is a simple, easy, and natural sound. It may increase in volume as emotions are in the process of release.

No special vocal technique is involved. There is no forcing of these sounds, and no thinking ahead about which sounds, or vowels, to use. Breathing is an integral part of Sounding. Attention to how to breathe to fill the lungs is essential.

Even those who may consider themselves to be non-singers may be able to make spoken sounds which are also suitable for Sounding.

Practice: Inhale. On the exhale, make a singing tone or sound, or a spoken sound, without using any melody or words, just a simple long sound or tone carried on the exhalation of your breath. Remember, there needs to be no forcing of these sounds, nor is it necessary to think ahead about which sounds or which vowel will be used. Allow the sounds to simply happen in the moment. Let your sound last for as long as your breath does. Then inhale again and make another sound. This sound may be higher or lower than the previous sound, and it may use a different vowel. (Often the spoken vowels come out naturally as ah, ee, i, o, or oo.)

Continue to make these elongated sounds for the duration of the breath, usually one sound for one breath. There will be a sense of when to stop, probably after about a half-minute or so, depending on your sense of closure.

As you become more practiced in Sounding this way, your sounds may grow stronger and last a little longer, as your breathing may become deeper and last longer. Because you are making sounds for their vibrational frequencies that blend with the thought of your intention, which also has vibrational frequencies, this blending of frequencies brings about some of the changes you intend. Powerful.

If you can speak, you can do Sounding (unless certain impairments prevent you from making sound). Remember: sounding is not about singing. This usage of your voice is not at all like singing, where the singer consciously manipulates the sounds for artistic effect. Sounding is not an artistic event meant for public performance. You are simply making the sounds that your human voice is capable of making, using your own particular voice's sounds, your vocal tones. Sounding is just allowing the vocal sounds to arise from within your body, automatically, or intuitively, not forcing the sounds by sheer dint of willpower. You do not have to think about which sound or vowel you will use. It is but a release.

Here is what actually happens, briefly, as you practice Sounding: Upon exhalation, your breath goes over your vocal cords in your throat (energy) causing these muscular folds to vibrate (vibration), which then activates the breath or air in the pharynx, your upper throat, above the cords. This air begins to vibrate at the same rate as the cords (frequency). You open your mouth, and the sound is sounded (sonic resonance). You have created energy, vibration, frequency, sound or sonic resonance. This is Sounding.

To demonstrate again for yourself, take an easy breath in. Begin to make your sound, paying attention to what is happening, but also do not do anything else to adjust what is happening, and do not do anything else to adjust what your body is doing. You and your body simply take in and release this breath and sound. Continue to make the sound. One sound may begin to take up the store of breath you have breathed in, so set up a rhythm of one sound lasting for one breath's intake. You do not have to decide which sound to make, because you are allowing the sounds to arise automatically and intuitively from your body.

You may be thinking, "I don't know what I am doing in this practice. Is this the right way?" It is simply a thought. There is no right or wrong way, actually. Observe this thought, but do not hang on to it or get into a discussion with yourself. Allow the idea to pass out of your awareness. Observe anything else that comes into your thoughts and let them go.

We are not interested in making melodies, just in simple vocal tones as softly or as loudly as they arise unaided from you. Different? Yes, this is the way to make sound for Sounding.

Important: before we begin to make the sounds, we make an intention. While we will explore intention in more detail later, for now for practice's sake, here is an example intention: go ahead and ask that your heart speak to you of something you want to heal or to understand better; this may come as an idea or as an image. Tell yourself that your body has its own consciousness, and it is to be trusted implicitly to do the very best for you and to maintain you in a state of health. Your body informs you in a variety of ways when it and you are inclined towards a certain state of distress or discomfort, long before any kind of illness manifests in the body. Sounding can be a tool for helping you to become alert to this kind of signal.

Listen with your inner awareness, as if you are listening on a phone with a bad connection to someone you truly wish to hear. That someone is *you*.

Your inner voice may be telling you, by means of your thoughts, what kind of experiences you are setting up for yourself. For instance, is your inner voice telling you that you will get stiff if you are sitting here too long? Then you most likely have a belief that stiffness occurs when the body is kept from moving over a certain period of time. You may experience stiffness after a while.

This is an example of how our thoughts make up our daily life for us. They are usually based on what we believe about our life and the reality we experience daily. So become aware of what you house in your head. If you find an idea you do not need now, or that no longer makes sense in view of your more mature understanding of yourself and the world, make an effort to change it into something that makes more sense now as you make your sounds. Or gently take the limiting idea that you have just discovered, hold it in your thoughts, turn it over, and examine it. As you do this, be alert to how you are feeling, as you think your idea through. Are you slightly annoyed by what the thought makes you do, or how it has you reacting? Does anger rise up in you?

Allow the natural vocal sounds you make to go with this feeling. Let them out. Be careful not to engineer the sounds. Let them be as they come out, as your response to your thought or idea.

When you come to the natural end of making sounds (you will sense when to stop) it is important that you stay with the silence for some time to allow the sounds to do their work.

You may feel your body tingling or feel energized in some way. Allow this. It is your body's response to the sounds. You have been reminding your body's cells of the sound qualities they need in order to be in health. In other words, you most likely made sounds that your cells need to 'hear'. You emitted frequencies that cause the cells to respond, to resound or resonate with health and balance. Or, saying it in another way, you energize your body with sound, lifting the frequencies to a higher rate of vibration needed to maintain a healthy cell where a cell may be 'out of tune' with itself.

All you have to do is intend, breathe, and make sound.

If at first you can only make a little sound, and only on maybe one or two levels of sound high or low, that is quite normal. Some people feel all they can do is sigh or hum at the beginning. After a while of practicing Sounding and becoming more relaxed with it, you will start to make sounds that surprise you in their scope or range or in actual volume, and many times, beauty.

There is no sense of judgment of how you sound, because it is your unique way of Sounding as you release what it is you need to let go of at the time. You may only be able to let the breath release from your body before there is much sound. There are no rules. You are in your private world expressing. It takes time for some people to get close enough to this way of observing themselves before they can utter anything like sounds. In time you will learn to modulate these responses to a more mellifluous sound.

Remember that you do not have to 'make up' the sounds, but there is nothing to stop you from intuiting them. With practice, you will realize that intuiting sounds is the ideal way of discovering what is inside waiting to be released. The sounds will come automatically, magically.

Sounding, when properly used, is effective even in difficult cases. Be playful with the practice, and yourself. Taking it too seriously impedes the intuitive flow of thoughts, feelings, and sounds. If, however, during a Sounding you find yourself in the throes of a deeply moving or disturbing storm, simply release the breath. With each release of the breath comes a corresponding inhalation, creating a slower rhythm, which you can use to come to a calmer place within yourself.

This is a detailed overview, and it may seem like too much information for you right now.

Just keep it for later, as you begin to move through the Explorations. Before you begin each one, your journey will be enhanced so much if you go to your Quiet-mind (see below, 'How do I get into Quiet-mind?), or go into a meditation state or a prayerful place that is comfortable for you. These states allow you to get the ego out of your way so that it will not influence your thinking.

How does Sounding work?

Match the frequency of the reality you want to experience, and that is what you get.
—*A possible attribution of Albert Einstein.*

In Sounding we are attempting to do what is said in this quote above and we will begin to unpack this idea.

As you now realize, this is not a book about how to sing. Nor is it a kind of self-help therapy book wherein you might be encouraged to yell, shout, scream or wail out your feelings. That is an expression of the ego. In Sounding we go into the intuitive self.

What is *intuitive* or *intuition*? Intuition is the ability to know or understand something without any conscious reasoning. You simply know. Perhaps you may have been thinking of someone you know, and quite soon you get a communication of some kind from them or about them. Or you just seem to know who is contacting you before you even pick up your phone. These are examples of intuition, a skill you may already have, in which case, you will find making sounds for Sounding easy or a skill that will develop as you go through the Explorations in part 2 of this book.

Let us begin to 'unpack' that quote from physicist Einstein, because this is an accurate description of what we do in Sounding, in our own way. We intend that our sounds are accepted by the cells of the body to be an accurate match for the cells' own vibrational frequency, in a healthy state and thus, creating wellbeing. Each cell in our body has its own vibrational frequency in good health.

When we get out of sorts, not feeling in optimal health, our cells vibrate at a lower rate of frequency than in health. In a laboratory setting, cancer cells have been shown to disintegrate when sound at a certain frequency is applied to them. With Sounding, we attempt in our way with our vocal sounds to restore health to our cells, not to destroy them. We are using sound frequencies to target the cells of our body that are not vibrating at their optimal frequency for good health, and we are at the same time using our thoughts, in our intention, to target these cells with our vocal sounds. Our thoughts direct the sound vibrations.

What is frequency?

Everything is Energy.
—Albert Einstein.

Energy is always moving, causing everything to be in a state of vibration of some kind. A prime resonance, or vibratory rate, is the rate at which something vibrates; it is how frequently that something vibrates. A slow vibrational frequency causes a low sound. Striking a big bass drum causes a slow vibrational frequency and so a low sound is produced. A faster vibrational frequency causes a higher sound, as a plucked string of a violin or guitar.

Remember, you are much more than your body. You are also mind and spirit, or soul. With the higher understanding of the inner self, you will intuit the correct frequency to change the vibrational frequency of a cell. You allow the sound to arise from within your body, and the sound "plays" your cells.

What is the reality you want to experience?

This is your intention for the Sounding you are about to make: what it is that you want in your life. By intending to do something or having the desire for a particular outcome, you direct your thoughts and ideas of action to bring about a certain event or thing into your experience. This is *the reality that you want.*

Using an intention when Sounding, you direct the intuitively made sounds into your body's cells that are not resonating at their prime resonance, or prime vibratory rate. These sounds find their way to the "out-of-tune" parts of you, but also, of your emotional body, of your mental body, and of your spiritual body.

Have you heard the story of the grandfather clocks which illustrates, for us, the mechanism by which our cells respond to the vibrations of our voices in Sounding?

Imagine a room filled with grandfather clocks, the ones that are set in long wooden cases, and which have long metal pendulums suspended from the clocks. Now, one of these pendulums is set in motion, swinging from left to right. You, as observer, will notice that soon each of the other clocks will alter their own motion to begin to swing left to right, synchronizing the movements of their pendulums with that of the original clock's pendulum. In Sounding, our cells behave in a similar way.

Keep your intention simple, clear, and achievable. For example: I intend that, during this Sounding, some of the tension in my neck is released, and that I learn some of the reasons for the tension, or perhaps how I feel about it.

We focus on our body because it is where we store our feelings, our deep emotions. If we do not come to terms with these deep, stored emotions, we run the risk of developing illnesses, mild or serious.

In Sounding, you are not focusing on finding a cure for the biggies—heart attacks, cancer, etc. —that persist in our world, although not impossible. Just keep it simple, focus on one simple imbalance at a time, such as something that is in your daily life that needs your attention to clear it.

In order to achieve a state of well-being, you need to trust that it can happen, but not to be concerned with the 'how' or 'why'; simply surrender to the outcome. This is self-care.

If even some of your many, many trillions of cells have 'slipped' from a proper healthy prime resonance, (their own self-tone which is the sound for them to be resonant with their healthy state) they become discordant, out-of-tune, so to speak. A negative or self-deprecating thought or feeling held briefly or for longer can cause this slipping. When this happens, other nearby cells may begin to resonate and vibrate with these cells. Then you begin to feel out of sorts or ill until these cells begin again to move into their prime resonance.

By intuitively making the sounds that the tiny cells vibrate to in well-being, as do those cells around them, these cells then pick up the resonance of the sounds from you and are restored to their own prime resonance. You are more than your body, which is the Seat of the Soul.

This is Sounding. This is matching the frequency of the reality you want to experience.

How do you know if your intention is working?

Do not keep looking for changes. This puts a different energy into the mix, while the vibrations from your voice, during the Sounding, attempt to match the vibrations of what you want to experience. During your day, remind yourself of your intention. Be a bit forceful and intense in your desire, then let it go. Do not dwell on it at all. Trust in the process.

This, as Einstein suggests, is matching the frequency you want. Tricky, you say? Yes, but you are guided by your inner self in this work. Little by little you begin to see things differently. Of course, there might be a sudden shift. It can occur, but not usually.

Did you get clear on what it is that you want to experience?

Remember the Cosmic Law: You cannot alter the experience of another person.

In other words, you cannot intend anything that may alter the life of anyone else.

That is interference. Not allowed.

You could, though, intend that your own experience of that person shifts to be more congenial. This is a subtle distinction, yes, but most important.

How do we access our feelings during Sounding?

During any one of the following Explorations, you may feel an emotion come up which you thought long buried but can be stimulated by your intention. If it seems right for you, allow it to surface. The emotion may be accompanied by a color, shape, idea, or a thought; observe these reactions. They are pointing you to something important. The feeling may have changed since you originally felt this emotion or the situation that caused it. How does this situation seem to you now? Send a little of your heart's love to this source and tell it you are no longer so fearful of it (if you are, perhaps you might want to seek the services of a trained professional), and you are willing at a later stage to more fully examine this emotion. No hurry on this. Later will do. Do only what feels comfortable to you right now as you are Sounding. Or do nothing. You are always in charge and always safe in this space. It is you that you are investigating, after all.

This is how we access our emotions during a Sounding session. Emotions are usually accompanied by a belief that you didn't know you had or had forgotten. As we said earlier, look at this belief, and, if you can, identify it and see if it is still worth keeping. If not, let it go. Replace it with one that is more helpful to you at this stage of your life. Changing a belief is as easy as that: think of one more suitable to you and put your energy and attention into the new belief. Notice your emotional state at this moment. Has there been a change, ever so slightly? Are you more comfortable now?

Take comfort in the limits of some ideas if those limits serve your greater good at this time. Whatever your feelings, give your body permission to take a test ride on Sounding Out Your Feelings!

Explore these ideas further at your own leisure. You might like to keep a journal on your thoughts and feelings—it's a wonderful way to keep track of your progress. You will soon become more acutely aware of your own needs and desires for change and growth, as you examine your conscious mind in this way. Sounding helps you get in touch with needs and desires to release what is not supporting you in health and happiness, and to bring in new ideas and thoughts which will support you to find a fuller expression of yourself as a human being.

Sounding can be a way of inviting in creative ideas when you feel blocked or stuck. These Explorations suggest a framework for your own future explorations into your own concepts of who and what you believe you are. Allow yourself to be comfortable with what you do at all times during the following Explorations, even when the experience gets a bit irksome. You are always in charge!

How do I get into Quiet-mind?

When you picked up this book and perhaps scanned it to learn what it was about, maybe you noticed that with each stand-alone Exploration I asked you to come with me to explore some part of your inner self, your psyche. Quiet-mind is a simple technique to enter through the doorway to this inner self. As part of the Sounding Out Your Feelings format, I began by asking you to come with me into quiet mind, or to use your own meditation technique to take yourself into a light trance state for best results with this kind of work. What, in fact, I am suggesting, is that you turn from your everyday awareness of your world to a deeper part of you that is, in essence, shifting your awareness to another part of your brain: the Alpha brainwave state. This is where creative people go when they are in the act of creating. Sometimes they acknowledge this state as being *in the zone*. Here we are simply turning away from everyday concerns to a personal space where you may more easily examine some place where you hold emotions that hurt or hinder your progress to being a more fulfilled human being. Whether you would like to learn a new technique for going into the Alpha state, or just need one for the purpose of Sounding, I will suggest an adaptation of a well-known way that I find usually successful:

After you have taken several slow, deep breaths as directed in each Exploration, come to this point where you begin to concentrate on a single focal point: your breathing.

> Begin by counting to three as you inhale through your nose, then hold your breath for the count of three, and slowly count three as you exhale through your slit lips.

Hold your breath once again for the count of three.

Repeat for as long as it takes for you to feel you are entering a light trance— just a small shift much like going into the sleep state before you fall asleep, or when you take a break from a difficult task to rest your brain.

Remain here in this state for Sounding Out Your Feelings in your selected Exploration.

When you want to come out of this light trance state, simply take a deep breath, open your eyes, and stretch, and bring your bodily senses back to your waking state:

Taste: roll your tongue around inside your mouth.

Smell: lift your hand to your nose and sniff it, for instance.

Touch: feel the fabric of your clothing.

Sight: look around you.

Hearing: listen to the sounds in your immediate environment.

A plan for Sounding Out Your Feelings sessions:

Become acquainted with your chosen Exploration's material. Alter it to suit your intention. Memorize it, if you like, or record it on your phone to play back when doing your chosen Exploration. Make your intention simple and clear. Go to your quiet mind.

Go a little deeper into your prayer state, or your meditation state, or Quiet-mind, with the breathing technique outlined above. Then going on with the Exploration of your choice, holding your intention in some part of your awareness, with the expectation that you will be successful, to some degree. Begin now to allow the sounds to arise automatically and magically from within you. Feel the wonder and miracle of your sounds as they come up out of the silence. Let the sounds be what they may for as long as you like, but do not tire your throat.

When you come to the natural completion of the sounds, be quiet and remain in your quiet mind state and maintain the silence. Here you may see lights, colors, shapes or images, or have thoughts related to your intention. All of these can be hints or clues to what may be a possible solution to your intention, or they may lead to where you could begin to make the changes you want.

When you feel it is time to return to your everyday world, breathe easily, stretch if you like, and open your eyes, and as suggested above, bring your physical senses back online. Sit quietly for a few moments, so that you are fully back to your daily reality.

This is how to practice a session of Sounding Out Your Feelings.

A word about your intention: the more intensely you visualize what it is that you want to experience (an event or anything), and the more intensely you feel about this intention, the better chance of this coming into play in your life. Another vital part of this is your expectation of success.

Let's go exploring!

PART 2

Exploring the Inner Landscape of Your Creative and Imaginative Feeling Self

EXPLORATIONS 1 – 8

Beginning the Grand Tour:

Sounding on your own to explore your relationship with yourself, the world within, and the world without

EXPLORATION 1:
Your Journey Begins

Come!

Let us go together

to explore the landscape of your inner self.

I am a guide who will show you the way

to find wonders you never dreamt existed before

which form portions of you—

a 'you' that expands into a vast hinterland of existence,

of experience, of ever-changing symbols, events,

sights, colors, smells, shapes, sounds, feelings.

I am like Mercury: playful, a magician, a wizard,

a sorcerer, a poet, a musician,

a singer of charms and spells!

I will teach you some of my secrets,

that you might fly on wings of sound

to those inner reaches of yourself that

are a universe—multilayered, multidimensional,
micro-cosmic, macro-cosmic, realms unknown,
or just thinly disguised illusions,
where exist your terror and fears,
your joys and sorrows,
your limits and boundaries,
your dearest wishes and hopes,
your deepest loves and passions,
your most hateful hating.

I will show you places to go in yourself
where you may bathe in the healing unction
of love and self-approval.

You may find pathways to allow yourself
to express all of these as you wish,
and to create a new place where you can live
in ease and comfort with yourself and who you
are becoming as you and I travel a little way together
on your magnificent adventure of living your life
as you want to live it,
and as you feel impelled from within!

Every journey begins with a breath.

Be in the present moment with your breath.

Close your eyes

and come with me

to the place just outside

the entranceway to your mind

and let us be here a little while

to consider what we are about to do.

Allow your body to be at ease.

Allow your breathing to be quiet and even.

Feel the direction of your breath as you bring it into your body—

through the nostrils, down your throat, and into your lungs.

Feel the breath as you breathe it gently out again with lips slightly parted.

For the next few breaths, be present, mindful of your breathing, as you observe

any ideas and thoughts coming in and taking up space in your mind.

Just watch them as they leave without taking up residence there.

Calmly and willingly let go of them.

With the exhalation of each breath, notice now

how your body is beginning to feel more at ease, your heart rate settles down, and tensions loosen.
You are coming into Quiet-mind.
Remain here during your Sounding Out Your Feelings session.

And, we are here at the Gateway to your mind,
and we begin to find the way through that entrance.
Ready now. We are at the portal.

For me, as your fellow traveler and tour guide,
this is an exciting moment,
to be here at the portal with you,
at this entranceway to your creative and imaginative feeling self.
How will you open this portal, this entranceway?
Your sounds, which I will soon direct you to use for this purpose,
will open it and your Sounding will carry you through it, if you truly want it,
and if you are willing to go the distance using your own voice,
whatever you think it sounds like, to take these steps to make those changes

in yourself that you want. What you do then is up to you.

How you use your emotions—only you can know this.

However, I am here to guide you with my voice through words.

I have traveled a way on my own and know some of the pitfalls and byways,

having encountered a few in my own inner self. I am happy to share my findings

with you that they may make your searching a little easier.

EXPLORATION 2:

The Keepers at the Gateway to Your Mind—and the filters through which you see the world and operate in it

Now, who are these "keepers," and how do they hinder entry into your mind and inner self? How do you recognize them? Protest though you may, you have put them there. They are the thought creations, ideas, and beliefs you hold that form the filters through which you see yourself and how you operate in the world around you. Consciously, or not, you are responsible for the existence of your filters. You continually recreate them, allowing them, without a moment's consideration, perhaps, to their appropriateness in your life at this present moment. In other words, you play those old thoughts on a loop over and over. Maybe you believe them so thoroughly, you do not suspect that you could be mistaken about them.

> We all do this to some degree or other.
>
> And maybe, just maybe, it never enters your mind that there might be an alternate view.

We wonder why our lives get in a mess, sometimes. The old rule is:

You get what you concentrate on.

By playing over those old thoughts on a loop, reconvincing ourselves of their rightness, we eventually recreate in our lives those very situations and events, or perpetuate newer ones, which hurt us and which we come to despise.

So, what's to be done? Things really don't change; do they?

"It would take a miracle to get me out of this mess." Heard that one before?

I did say I would teach you my secrets!

This is a secret that you already know deep in your heart.

I am simply reminding you that you know this in some part of yourself:

Change your thoughts and you change your life.

This is a beginning. So, as we progress through these Explorations, you will have opportunities to examine many of your beliefs about yourself and your ways of expressing in the world. You will find opportunities to change those you wish to change through riding on the sounds of your own voice and your intention for such change.

Let us stop that old thinking and take a look at what some of it is saying to you. Is the title for your first thought, "Let me count the ways I despise myself?"

Would you, perhaps, consider for a moment some of the ways you would like to think of yourself and how others might perceive you?

There is no charge for this. No penalty. You may do it freely and for as long as you wish. It may be an indulgence to think well of yourself, so perhaps you are not so ready to do it. It is fine. Go ahead—do it. You could make your intention here to understand yourself a little better, beginning with your image of your own body. Think, for instance, of one part of your body which you secretly really like, or even better, love. Look at that part of yourself (is it your hair or your hands, for instance?) and tell yourself that you do indeed like or love it.

Now, with this feeling of loving this part of yourself still clear in your feelings awareness, let us, with this new clarity, come just a little bit closer to the two keepers at the Gateway to your mind.

> Keeping your eyes closed, and being in the present moment with your breath:
>
>> Come with me to the place just outside
>>
>>> this entranceway to your mind, and let us be here a little while
>>
>>>> and consider what we are about to do.

Allow your body to be at ease.

allow your breathing to be quiet and even, as you come closer to Quiet-mind.

Feel the direction of your breath as you bring it into your body—

through the nostrils, down your throat, and into your lungs.

Feel the breath as you gently breathe out with lips slightly parted.

For the next few breaths, be present, mindful of your breathing,

as you watch any ideas and thoughts that may come in and take up space in your mind.

Just watch them as they leave, without taking up residence there.

Calmly and willingly let go of them.

With the exhalation of each breath, notice now how your body

feels more at ease, and your heart rate settles down, tensions loosening.

You are coming into Quiet-mind.

Remain here during your Sounding.

We are here at the entranceway to your mind through your body, and here we begin to find the way through that entranceway.

As you continue to feel at ease, be present in the moment with your breath,

paying attention to the act of breathing.

With your intention in some part of your awareness, and your body still and relaxed,

see in your imagination a clearer picture of this Gateway to your mind.

Let us together look beyond the two keepers to see what is there.

We see a beautiful summer garden.

There is a path winding amongst the flowers and green shrubs,

let us wander along it in our imagination.

Smell the scents from the blooms around us,

and feel the warm sunshine on your arms,

and your hair gently blowing around your face

as the breeze moves through the bushes and branches.

At the end of the path is a wrought-iron arched gate

with roses climbing over the arch in red profusion.

As we move closer, see that the gate is finely wrought filigree through which you see glimpses of what is beyond:

tantalizing jigsaw-puzzle pieces, interesting and colorful,

kaleidoscopic fragments of the multi-potential you.

As you look at these, feel your breath coming into your body,

refreshing you.

As you exhale, let a sigh ride out on your breath.

On the next two or three breaths allow your sighs

to become longer and filled with sound,

until they are louder sounding.

You are revving-up your vocal mechanism

in preparation for our journey through the arched gate

to your inner self.

As your sounds relax you into ease,

look more closely,

you can just sense now, rather than see,

the presence of those two forms

standing on either side of the Gateway.

Ask yourself if you are willing to look further, to find out

who or what these forms are and represent to you.
Friend or foe?
Ask yourself if you are made afraid by their presence,
or if they feel familiar, as old friends do.

This is a good time to learn what your body can tell you about
what you are feeling. Check the pit of your stomach,
for you know how that feels when you are afraid.
You also know how it feels to be glad around the heart area.
Explore other feelings if you like.
Perhaps make a mental "feelings file," and keep these feelings there for future reference.
Are you maintaining your breathing and long-sounding pattern?
Still hold your intention in some part of your awareness.
But focus your attention now on the form to the left of the Gateway.
Invite this presence to come towards you a step or two.
This presence feels familiar to you and not scary,

and you wish to know why it is guarding this place.

You somehow recognize it. It is a version of yourself from the past,

the one who holds limiting ideas about you that you

are beginning to notice and not like.

This is your time to dialogue with this self

to discover what changes you can and want to make together

to become the person you want to be in the future, and

to love who you are in your present moment.

The slow, even breathing and varied long-sounded tones will assist you and carry you through the maze of emotions which may arise as you meet with yourself over these matters in this and in later Explorations. Ride with the Sounding as it goes through your body, and let it become the expression of your feelings!

At this point, you may sound like a banshee wailing, or like a child whimpering. There may be tears, too. Perhaps some will be joyful tears: you are, at last, confronting your ideas and feelings about yourself in this safe way. Whatever your feelings, they are expressing through your body and those vocal sounds of yours. Those noises are valid. Let them be what they are, for now. Don't judge them or attempt to change them. That would be a form of denial of who you are. Your aim here is to get at the true expression of your feelings. No holds barred.

You may sound like a diva—or just a moan! With practice, you will begin to make vocal tones that are most effective, and sometimes beautiful. Make your sounds, whatever it takes to Sound Out Your Feelings.

Take as much time as you need. You will come to a natural place of ease and peace as this sounds itself out. You may not yet have a clear idea of what you are expressing with Sounding. However, you will know the general issue or the area you are working in.

When you do come into the natural silence after the noisy storm, stay here a while, breathing naturally and deeply, easily, remaining in Quiet-mind. You are allowing the molecules and cells of the body to settle into a more comfortable place after the vibrational shower you have just given them. This is when the healing takes place.

You and your body will feel more soothed and comforted than before the Sounding while in this silence. You may find that ideas, thoughts, images, symbols, or colors are coming freely into your awareness, so aim to catch a few for closer examination. They may be clues to what your sounds have been expressing.

Now bring your attention for a moment to the presence on the left side of the Gateway. This journey into your inner landscape will determine just who this one will be when you move through the Gateway back to the everyday world.

> When you are ready, inhale and exhale, open your eyes, and stretch.
>
> Bring your outer senses back online:
>
> Taste: roll your tongue around the inside your mouth.
>
> Smell: lift your hand to your nose and sniff it, for instance.
>
> Touch: feel the fabric of your clothing.
>
> Sight: look around you.
>
> Hearing: listen to the sounds in your immediate environment.
>
> You are back in your everyday world.

Each Exploration that you make, and the changes that occur, will influence the outcome as you grow into your future self, to the one you are going to be able to love unconditionally, as you would love a beloved pet. You gradually move into being someone whom you can personally like, without your expectations placed upon what kind of a person you are, or how you think others see you, simply just because you are, like a lovely flower blooming.

> If you feel ready, you can go on up to the Gateway—It's open.
>
> Your Sounding Out Your Feelings was the key to unlocking it.
>
> Taking a look through costs nothing. You can come this far as many times as you like.
>
> This next Exploration offers you the opportunity to take just one look.

EXPLORATION 3:
The Dragon of Illusion:
How you see yourself through the eyes of others

You have successfully used the key of Sounding to open the Gateway to your inner world during Exploration 2, and now you are here ready to take a look around, which is all it has to be if that is all you feel up to doing at this time.

> So, let us take some initial steps.
>
> Be in the present moment with your breath.
>
> Close your eyes and come with me
>
> to the place just outside the Gateway to your mind,
>
> and let us be here a little while
>
> to consider what we are about to do.
>
> Allow your body to be at ease.
>
> Allow your breathing to be quiet and even, deepening to your Quiet-mind.

Feel the direction of your breath as you bring it into your body—

through the nostrils, down your throat, and into your lungs.

Feel the breath as you gently exhale through slightly parted lips.

For the next few breaths, be present and mindful.

Watch any ideas and thoughts as they come in and take up space in your mind.

Just watch them as they leave, without taking up residence there.

Calmly and willingly let go of them.

With the exhalation of each breath, notice now how your body

is beginning to feel more at ease.

Your heart rate settles down and tensions loosen.

You are coming to Quiet-mind. Begin Sounding now.

From this place, come with me closer to the Gateway

to observe what we can see beyond it.

Are you ready to explore?

Make your intention to know more of this dragon

of illusion.

See yourself going through the open Gateway.

It is not locked, but will open easily when you want to return

to the physical world once again after Sounding.

Here's the idea: when you feel you have had enough of Exploring,

when it gets too close to the bone,

or when it seems you have triggered a response in your

emotions too hot to handle for now,

simply inhale deeply and, as you exhale,

open your eyes and stretch your body, breathe, and bring your

outer senses back online.

For now, if you are feeling brave enough,

let us proceed to look around.

Continue to hold, in some part of your awareness, your intention and

your breathing and Sounding patterns as you allow your mind's eye to gaze about.

You are now becoming aware of being in a beautiful garden set in an atrium.

The walls of this place are made of translucent brick

through which you can make out mottled colors of things beyond.

You are protected here. It is quiet and peaceful.

Check through your senses for perfumes from the flowering bushes.

Listen for sounds of birds, of waterfalls, or of distant music.

Examine things by casting your gaze around you.

Look up now, and notice that there seems to be a mist above the garden,

and there are double glass-like doors ahead of you.

Go take a peep through the mist and those glass doors.

That mist is also outside beyond the atrium.

It is okay to open the doors.

You don't have to go through them if that is what you choose;

just stay here looking out for a while.

You are comfortable, at home.

It is somehow familiar to you,

yet you feel a slight sense of uneasiness; something doesn't quite fit.

This might puzzle you a bit, so let us take only a step outside,

and you may keep hold of the door if you like, while we examine

the feeling of being one step beyond comfortable, familiar territory.

The mist circles above your head and around your face in soft whispers.

It is so gentle you almost don't feel it.

You sense others standing around out in this misty place.

Look down at your feet. You can clearly see the ground where you stand.

You are secure and balanced. There is no threat from these others;

they, too, are familiar to you.

They are the people in your life at this present time.

Look up once again.

Some of those faces are becoming recognizable. Ah, yes,

you know them all too well; they have been part of your life—

parents, grandparents, uncles, aunts, sisters, brothers, cousins,

best friends, good friends, acquaintances, teachers,

or any others who represent authority figures in your life.

You know who these people are for you, because they interact daily

in your thought patterns of how you see yourself expressing in the world

as you move through your day.

They affect your life in some way or another by being there.

They reflect back to you how you see yourself. They may have plenty to say.

Yet they need to say nothing at all to you for them to have a definite impact on how you behave.

It is how you perceive what others expect of you
that creates your actions and behavior when you
let those expectations work on you.

Recall the intention for this Sounding regarding
how you would truly like to be thought of
by some of these people in your life, and ask
yourself: what is this dragon of illusion?

In these Explorations we are going to examine
some of these relationships.

Your own feelings towards others, for example,
are a direct reflection

of what you feel and think about yourself.

If you love yourself and like yourself, you will
attract love and liking from others.

The people in your life who cannot reflect this
back to you may fall away

from contact with you or be outside of your
awareness.

Others who can love and like you will surround
you,

and be the kind of people you can like and love,

because they, too, are likable and lovable.

These familiar faces in your life are no threat—you've heard

their admonishments all before; you know what they expect from you.

You may dislike them, but you pretty much know what to expect from them.

You have managed to erect some walls around yourself regarding them,

so that you can handle daily living. You find your comfort zone in all of this.

Yet that is exactly what bugs you—the fact that you have to erect such walls.

You wish to be free of their expectations of you.

The mist still circles around you,

and your breathing and Sounding pattern

needs some attention from you. Are you breathing slowly and gently?

Allow your sounds to be what they want to be right now.

Do you want to know the source of this mist? It is *you*.

You are playing the role of dragon of illusion.

You breathe the mist of illusion around yourself.

This mist helps create so much going on in your life that you

end up locked in the roaring confusion of the events of life,

feeling powerless to alter anything.

The illusion is: that you are powerless.

The illusion is: that what others expect of you is what you have to do.

You may be afraid of being called selfish by those who may be masters

at this powerplay over you.

See it this way: You can do what is best for you, first.

It may be a new and uncomfortable idea for you.

Explore the feelings that come up with this idea.

Allow your sounds to rise up in you to reflect this feeling.

Sound for as long as it feels necessary or natural.

When you come to this natural silence after

Sounding Out Your Feelings,

let your thoughts and feelings be your clues to how you can claim back your power

to make clear decisions about what is best for you.

When you are ready, inhale and exhale, open your eyes, and stretch.

Bring your outer senses back online.

You are back in your everyday world.

EXPLORATION 4:
Resounding in the Corridors of Power

While you made your way through Exploration 3, the mists of illusion began to clear, along with some of your feelings and ideas about who's in charge of you and your life, and you may feel less like the impotent raging dragon of illusion that you may, perhaps, have felt yourself to be in the past. Some of your ideas about how you can operate in the world are beginning to change, and you see other possibilities for action that are opening up for you to envision. There is yet much to discover about you that is creative and exciting.

> Be in the present moment with your breath.
>
> Close your eyes.
>
> Come with me
>
> to the place just outside
>
> the Entrance way to your mind,
>
> and let us be here a little while to consider what we are about to do.

Here make your intention.

Allow your body to be at ease.

Allow your breathing to be quiet and even, as you come towards Quiet-mind.

Feel the direction of your breath as you bring it into your body—

through the nostrils, down your throat, and into your lungs.

Feel the breath as you gently exhale through slightly parted lips.

For the next few breaths, be present, mindful of your breathing.

Watch any ideas and thoughts as they come in and take up space in your mind.

Just watch them as they leave, without taking up residence there.

Calmly and willingly let go of them.

With the exhalation of each breath,

you notice now how your body is beginning to feel more at ease.

Your heart rate settles down, and tensions loosen.

You are coming into Quiet-mind.

Remain here as you begin your Sounding.
And, riding on the long sounds with breath,
come through the Gateway to your inner being
and let's go adventuring!

Allow your sounds to grow into long sounds for the duration
of one breath, simply for as long as your breath lasts,
then take another breath and continue with your Sounding.
These sounds need not be loud to be effective.

Remember, if you can speak, you can do Sounding.
When you speak, you expect that your voice will happen,
to respond to you, as you begin to speak,
you do not make any kind of adjustments to make your voice
sound the words you wish to speak.
Sounding is made the same way.
You must simply expect those sounds to arise

from within your body,

intuitively, automatically, without fuss or adjustments.

By making your vocal sounds in this way you may even activate

overtones in each tone you make, although this is not necessary.

Overtones, or the harmonic series of higher sounds, are present and

active in all sounds of the voice, whether we can hear them or not.

They are to sound what the color spectrum is to light.

They enrich each sound you make by bringing in more vibrations.

We say, 'overtones color the sound of the voice.'

Let us go a little further,

on the wings of your sound,

through the little atrium garden.

Today it is sunny and flower-scented.

Go out through the glass doors,

which you allow to swing gently back into place,

knowing that you can easily return any time you wish.

The mists of yesterday in Exploration 3 are clearing.

You find yourself moving past those faces who had seemed

to hold you in the spells of their expectations of you.

They have far less hold on you now since you have begun

to be clear about what you want for yourself.

See how they move back to make a pathway for you to pass by?

They seem friendlier, more allowing of you.

Be mindful of your intention here

and that you are becoming more at ease with making your sounds.

Ahead of you, see a place that looks like a large public building.

It is dome-shaped and has steps leading up to the door.

You bound up the steps on your sound and enter into the domed hall.

It has wide corridors leading off into the interior of this place.

You see tall, wide pillars that look like pink marble rising up

from the floor of purple-pink marble (which may seem to be a

representation of your vocal cords).

Large round windows allow sparkling crystalline light to flood this space.

This light is so bright, you feel you are being filled with it.

And the light is sound, and it spills out of you, on your breath,

filling this wonderful space!

Allow your body to make sound as if it were a beautiful instrument, like a violin,

or a cello, or a trumpet, or whatever you prefer, as if it is being played by an angel.

Continue for as long as you wish—the longer the better.

When you come to the natural silence once again, remain still,

breathing easily, eyes closed. Remain in Quiet-mind.

Let yourself bask in the tingling dance of your molecules

as they find their right place of resonance in your body.

Listen to hear them singing and sounding their true tones for well-being.

When you are ready, inhale, exhale, open your eyes, and stretch.

Bring your outer senses back online –

You are back in your everyday world.

The longer time, say a few minutes, that you can devote to Sounding, the more you will feel the beneficial effects of being 'toned-up' and the more clearly your brain will function. You have just given it a massage, so to speak, with Sounding. More oxygen is getting into your bloodstream as you breathe deeply and evenly for the Sounding. Your whole body is enlivened and revitalized with breath and vocal tones.

Sounding can be a gentle high.

It is important to stay within the silence after Sounding, while remaining in Quiet-mind, so that you and your body can reap the benefits of the healing and balancing that occurs during this time.

Sound used in this way can act as a pathway to

other levels of consciousness, if you desire to go this route. You can also direct your vocal sounds to areas where you may be feeling twinges or aches and pains. Intuit the sound needed to restore balance and direct it allowing it to Sound Out any discomfort. Vocal sound is a great healer and restores well-being. Experiment and explore with sound to maintain your own sense of well-being.

EXPLORATION 5:
In the Hall of Mirrors

The world and those in it reflect back to yourself.

Close your eyes and come with me to the place

just outside the Gateway to your mind and inner self.

Let us be here a little while to consider what we are about to do.

Allow your body to be at ease.

Allow your breathing to be quiet and even, as you come towards Quiet-mind.

Feel the direction of your breath as you bring it into your body—

through the nostrils, down your throat, and into your lungs.

Feel the breath as you gently exhale through slightly parted lips.

For the next few breaths, be present, mindful of your breathing.

Watch any ideas and thoughts as they come in and take up space in your mind.

Just watch them as they leave without taking up residence there.

Calmly and willingly let go of them.

With the exhalation of each breath, notice now how your body

is beginning to feel more at ease. Your heart rate settles down, and tensions loosen.

You are coming into Quiet-mind.

Remain here during your Sounding.

Begin Sounding, and riding on your sound. Come once again through the Gateway

to your inner mindscape, and let's go adventuring!

As you sound, intend that you begin to see yourself as others do,

so that you may make some changes which you now feel are necessary.

Or create your own intention.

During your visit to the Corridors of Power where you experienced resonant sound, you had a taste of how it would be to feel in vibrant well-being.

Bring your imagination again to the front steps of this domed place.

This time, ascend the steps one at a time, in rhythm with your breathing.

On each step, listen for the tone of that step as it resonates in your body.

You may become aware of a corresponding color for each tone.

As you arrive up on the top step, look around you.

There are some doorways leading inward to the central hallway

where you first practiced making your sound.

Choose which doorway you will enter by.

In this domed hall you are comfortable; it is, by now, familiar to you.

Go in through your chosen doorway and allow your Sounding to arise

within you to a warm resonant tone,

as if you are the domed hall with corridors.

Your resonant sound carries you, as you imagine yourself moving towards the doorway of one of the corridors to check it out.

Are you ready to explore further?

Let your Sounding subside a little and just breathe normally.

Notice that the walls of the corridor reflect your image

as you pass by, and it seems as if you are accompanying yourself

on this little trip into your creative inner mindscape.

Be aware of your body responses-your heartbeat and pulse,

your breathing pattern, slow or fast or normal,

the pit of your stomach, or the area about and below your heart.

Remember how it feels to be glad around the heart area,

because there is nothing to fear in this place.

If you do feel a little concerned, ask yourself why.

Wait for a symbol, a picture, or image to show up to help you understand your body's feelings.

Notice now that many images reflect back to you from the walls of this place. Some seem familiar, others do not.

Those images that seem familiar to you are those aspects

of you that you recognize in others. You may like some and despise some.

Look at one of these reflected aspects of yourself.

Perhaps it is something about your mother that bugs you,

or perhaps it is something about someone else.

You know which it is that is currently working on you,

and who is reflecting it back to you.

Form your intention here regarding this person or aspect of them.

Continue Sounding Out Your Feelings as you contemplate this aspect.

Judge it not, nor praise it, but just let it be what it is

until it tells you what within you that can alter this situation.

Tricky, but be as honest as you can at this point.

Your Sounding will carry you right to the nub of the solution,

at least close enough for you to get the idea of

what you may want to change.

Be kind to yourself and others who reflect back to you.

Bless them, too; for these are truly some of the teachers in your life.

Allow yourself to come to the place of silence after your Sounding,

and rest here in the silence, still in Quiet-mind, feeling the healing power

of the sounds restoring you to comfort and ease with this part of yourself.

When you are ready, inhale and exhale, open your eyes, and stretch.

Bring your outer sense back online.

You are back in your everyday world.

EXPLORATION 6:
In the Land Where Every Wish is Granted: Mind what you think

Be in the present moment with your breath.

Close your eyes

and come again with me

to the place just outside the Gateway to your mind

and let us be here a little while to consider what we are about to do.

Allow your body to be at ease.

Allow your breathing to be quiet and even.

Feel the direction of your breath as you bring it into your body—

through the nostrils, down your relaxed throat, and into your lungs.

Feel the breath as you gently exhale through slightly parted lips.

For the next few breaths, be present, mindful of your breathing.

Watch any ideas and thoughts as they come in and take up space in your mind.

Just watch them as they leave without taking up residence there.

Calmly and willingly let go of them.

With the exhalation of each breath, notice now how your body

is beginning to feel more at ease. Your heart rate settles down. Tensions loosen.

You are coming into Quiet-mind.

Remain here during your Sounding.

Begin Sounding, and riding on your sounds,

come once more with me through the Gateway

to the mindscape of your inner self

and let's go adventuring!

I will take you now to a magical land

where every wish is granted!

Allow yourself to come with me, in your imagination, to this place I know.

It is called Terra, the land of physicality where whatever is thought of

is materialized into form, in some way.

Here, everything is possible, and probable.

You have so many probabilities to choose from,

you can easily become confused and make unwise choices.

It is not always a simple matter to recognize your creations,

because they can lose something in the translation to form

from imagination or thought.

This is due, in large part, to a lack of clarity in the image-maker.

Many who live in this land, Terra,

are not aware that they are image-makers,

or thought-manifesters.

This is where a lot of waste of energy takes place.

Objects and events are created for which no one takes credit, or responsibility.

Even some Terrans are created in this way.

Whether they are aware of it or not, those who inhabit this land of Terra

are here to learn how to become impeccable manifesters,

and to use thought-energy with utmost care, economy, and mindfulness.

One of the reasons why we are visiting here is to give you some training

in becoming an impeccable image-maker,

to learn how to bring into your life what you would like to experience.

Once again, it is both magical and simple.

Let me remind you of how to do this.

You already know about it,

but you have buried this deep inside yourself.

As you grew into adulthood you forgot it,

and too, you have forgotten just how easy it is.

All the children of Terra know this secret magical formula.

They do not have to be taught it from birth.

Although, like you, they tend to forget about it

as they grow up. The magic is here, nonetheless.

You get what you concentrate on.

This is the magic formula.

Oh, so you've heard this one before?

We can put it another way.

You create your own reality by what you think, feel, believe, and energize with your thoughts.

Remember those old thoughts going around and around in your head?

Same thing.

This is possibly one of the most important magical formulae

I can teach you to remember while in Terra.

Here is a twist to it that you may not have thought of:

Rather than just avoiding unpleasant events and people,

use this formula to attract into your life creative experiences for yourself

which will help you to expand your horizons, to make your life

more meaningful and enjoyable, and whatever else you would like.

There is a key to making this formula work:

you Intend what you want to have happen.

Yes. We have been here already.

How does Intending work?

Let us explore this intending idea. Intending implies success.

Wishing allows for a little failure. So does hoping.

Instead, you simply decide what it is that you want to experience,

imagine it and having it-with intensity and with the expectation

that you can have it show up in your life somehow.

Total trust that it will come helps with this intending game,

although it may not come in the form that you expected.

So, allow for this possibility when intending.

Inform the world, the universe, the powers that be,

the gods, God, whomever you call upon in your hour of need,

or whomever you hang out with in spirit,

that you are playing Intending and what it is that you intend.

You must know that you are completely worthy of receiving

this gift deep in your bones, no room for doubt.

You can have anything you want here in Terra,

provided it does no harm.

Contrary to what you may have been told,

there is nothing to feel guilty over, either.

One proviso: you cannot intend for anyone else.

That would constitute a violation of Cosmic Law.

As you move around here in Terra, remember this:

that you intend to go into the unknown in joy,

in harmony, peace, and safety.

Know this in your bones, also: Mind what you think.

What you think of has a funny way of showing up somehow.

Stay here as long as you wish. You know the way home.

Before you leave here, bring your thoughts to something

you would like to experience in your life.

Let us intend this and energize it with our Sounding.

Be aware of your breathing deep in your body

and state clearly in your mind what you intend to manifest.

Allow your sounds to form up, and allow your body to be played, as a fine instrument might be played, by the sounds, without

consciously arranging which sounds, or vowels, to be used.

See your sounds energizing the image you have of what it is that

you want to experience. This is matching the frequency.

See your sounds pouring into your image, fleshing it out,

making it as real to you as it can be.

Play with your sound as it plays with your body,

imagining your intention into life.

As mentioned, of course, things may not come out just as you thought they might,

but that is the nature of the Universe, and they may take a little time to show up.

Go into the place of silence letting the sound do its work.

Remain in Quiet-mind.

Be aware of colors, images, or feelings that come up during this silence.

When you are ready, inhale, exhale, open your eyes, and stretch.

Bring your outer senses back online.

You are back in your everyday world.

Learning to create the reality of your own life is the most important lesson of all of these Explorations that I can, as your guide, teach you! All else is "icing on the cake," nonetheless important, too. Cleaning out old attitudes and beliefs is important work; have no illusions.

EXPLORATION 7:
Playing as the Children of Terra: Your natural impulses lead you where you intend to go

Be in the present moment with your breath.

Close your eyes,

and come with me

to the place just outside

the entranceway to your mind

and let us be here a while to consider what we are about to do.

Bring yourself and your body to your place of stillness.

Allow your breathing to be quiet and even.

Feel the direction of your breath as you bring it into your body—

through the nostrils, down your throat, and into your lungs.

Feel the breath as you gently exhale through slightly parted lips.

For the next few breaths, be present, mindful of your breathing.

Watch any ideas and thoughts as they come in and take up space in your mind.

Just watch them as they leave without taking up residence there.

Calmly and willingly let them go.

With the exhalation of each breath, notice how your body is beginning

to feel more at ease. Your heart rate settles down and tensions loosen.

You are coming into Quiet-mind.

Remain here, in Quiet-mind during your Sounding.

Come with me as you begin to sound,

and riding on these sounds, come through the Gateway

to the inner mindscape of your deepest self.

Let's go adventuring!

Remember yourself as a child, a very small child.

Go into your first memory of yourself this young and how it feels to be so young.

Bring to mind your thoughts and emotions connected with this.

Some of us have memories we would rather not have.

If this is so, we will go on to a pleasant memory, or insert an invented one,

one when you felt protected, loved, and taken care of,

as carefree as only a child can feel who knows of nothing else.

You remember creating the magic that children do,

making things happen because that is the way you saw it,

believing it to be, expecting it to be.

You think it, and it is.

As an adult how can you possibly pursue this line of thinking,

and keep some kind of control of your life and appear sane and

normal to the rest of the world?

First of all, this is the land where wishes are granted, by you!

Once you make your intention and follow the ways set out in Exploration 6,

you will begin to notice little things catching your interest.

Maybe a book on your shelves will make itself obvious to you,

and you haven't looked at it in ages and maybe not at all since you bought it.

Yet something makes you open it, and lo and behold!

Right there on that page is something related to your intention.

You may think about a certain aspect of it.

Perhaps you will feel compelled to take a certain action based on your feelings as you read.

This in turn may lead you to another form of action which may be that you mention the book to a friend who just has a snippet of information regarding the author.

"That person is giving a lecture in town next week-would you like to come?" They ask.

The lecture supplies you with information related to your intention

which brings it nearer to manifesting in your life in some way.

And so, it goes on and on.

Following these little impulses leads you where you intend to go,

sometimes only realizing it in hindsight.

These things have a pattern to them, once you look back and let it show itself to you.

Sometimes impulses can take a different form.

You are in a playful mood and you want to slack,

and you cannot get started on that work that sits there waiting for your attention,

and you must have it ready by Tuesday. You experience a real block there.

You let your attention wander and find yourself daydreaming,

as you stare out the window at some children at play.

Without being fully aware of it happening,

you have been thinking, at another level of yourself,

of the project and you have mapped out the strategy and know the working plan for it.

Delighted, you get to work eagerly.

You followed your impulse to daydream, and it led to a solution.

If you follow these inclinations, or impulses from inner self,

they will always lead you to your highest good,

provided you are operating within your integrity towards that goal.

Bring your attention to your breathing and breathe deep in the body,

exhale and fill your head with the sweet resonance of your sounds

which energizes your intention as you form it at this moment.

Let your sound take you where it will, and be mindful of what images are

passing through the front of your mind's eye, your inner vision.

These are your clues to solutions embedded in your intentions.

Each successive present moment unfolds from this one.

Another way to see it is as the ever-expanding present moment.

Be attentive, be mindful, be in charge of what you think because thinking creates!

What are you feeling as you are Sounding?

Ride on your sounds wherever they will take you. They energize your intentions, and you,

knowing that if you are happier, those around you will benefit from this and will be affected by you loving yourself more.

Let the Sounding carry you to that place within where you are at ease and in comfort

at being who you are. Let the sounds be what they will be.

When you come to the natural silence, stay with the aftermath of the Sounding,

and remain in Quiet-mind. Allow your body to settle into balance and well-being,

your feelings coming to resolution,

and your mind clear in your intention.

When you are ready, inhale and exhale, open your eyes, and stretch.

Bring your outer senses back online.

You are back in your everyday world.

EXPLORATION 8:
If You Ruled the World:
Loving what you do for a living

Close your eyes and come with me

to that place just outside

the entranceway to your mind,

and let us be here a while to consider what we are about to do.

Bring yourself and your body to your place of stillness,

and allow your breathing to be quiet and even.

Feel the direction of your breath as you bring it into your body—

through the nostrils, down your throat, and into your lungs.

Feel the breath as you gently exhale through slightly parted lips.

For the next few breaths, be present, mindful of your breathing.

Watch any ideas and thoughts as they come in and take up space in your mind.

Just watch them as they leave without taking up residence there.

Calmly and willingly let them go.

With the exhalation of each breath, you notice now how your body

feels more at ease. Your heart rate settles down, and tensions loosen.

You are coming into Quiet-mind.

Remain here during your Sounding.

Begin your Sounding. Riding on long sound,

come through the Gateway again to the magical world of yourself,

and let's go adventuring!

Consider: if only I had …

If only I were rich …

If only all things were equal …

I could conquer the world!

At least I'd have a job that I liked.

I am not doing anything that seems

to be remotely meaningful.

For me. Or for my boss. Or for society.

It's just for the money, really.

I have to live somehow, pay the rent,

feed myself.

It's an old story often heard, right?

Is it yours, too?

Riding on the breath and sound,

let us go once more to the magical land of Terra.

See yourself in an ideal situation for you—

one where you are engaged in doing something you do well,

and that you like, even love, to do.

Maybe you sew clothes well.

Or perhaps you are artistic, and paint pictures,

or you make clever and witty jewelry pieces, or sculpt,

or maybe you make wonderful bread and baked goods.

Perhaps you have a green thumb,

and enjoy a good relationship with the garden devas,

and plants seem to flower and fruit with your very touch.

Perhaps you are clever with machines, repairing them,

or rebuilding them, or you have a talent for designing

and building unusual and useful things.

Whatever your talent is, whatever it is that you love to do well,

that is your own personal feeling-tone, that is how you feel yourself to be,

which is the sound of you as you resonate in the world, and in the universe.

When one does not listen to this feeling-tone,

when one is steered away from expressing it, from Sounding it out,

either by one's own fears, or by others' opinions or lack of support,

or the outright disagreement of others towards

one's true expression of talent, or abilities,

there is a blockage of energy, a dissonance, which may bring in its wake discomfort, disease,

and so on.

Deep in your heart you are aware of this ability, this talent.

The best way to recognize it, if you haven't already,

is to go to that place inside yourself where you have that feeling

that you might have been interested in doing whatever it is

(painting houses, making pottery, fixing computers, etc.).

You think you might have been rather good at it.

You have nimble fingers for working with small pieces

as in watchmaking, or tying knots in rugs, for instance.

Make the intention now, as you are Sounding and letting

your sounds express your feelings about this,

that you will allow yourself to have a glimpse of your talent,

your bent, your self-tone, your secret desire.

And know that you can recognize it with your conscious mind

as well as with your feeling self (which probably knows already

although you have not acknowledged it).

By now, you have gotten in touch with something in your secret heart,

because sound always gets to the point.

Be gentle with your sound,

For tears of recognition may flow freely,

and bring you to a place of calm, of quiet joy,

and of pleasure that you have at last unearthed this desire

through your intention.

Sound for as long as you need.

When you come to the silence, remain here in Quiet-mind,

as you firm up your intention to act upon this new self-discovery.

When you are ready, inhale and exhale, open your eyes, and stretch.

Bring your outer senses back online.

You are back in your everyday world.

By now you have come to some understanding that you do, indeed, rule your own private world of experience. It does take skill, care, and mindfulness to become an impeccable image-maker, creator of your own reality.

It does take courage, dear fellow traveler, to believe that it can be done, and that you can do it. And it does take willingness to take this risk to believe, and to begin to do it. However, the rewards are well worth the effort and the risk.

Decide which direction will best nurture your gift of your self-tone, and to follow your passion to the fulfillment of your creative and imaginative feeling self.

Doing what you love to do for your occupation provides you with a living, which has meaning and rewards for your efforts; it is not just a job, but becomes you, faithfully expressing yourself in the world.

At the beginning of these adventures I spoke about self-care, and again I stress how vital to your state of wellbeing in body, mind, soul, and heart this is. All that you have experienced in these past few years has had certain effects upon you—what you now think about, what you now feel you need in your life, how your emotions change and vary in a different way from before past events happened in the outer world.

We can examine some effects of these outer conditions as we venture further with these self-explorations to follow. Before we embark on the next stage of this incredible journey, ask yourself if you want to add anything else, or make up your own topics for future explorations relating to those already examined. These can be revealing as to how you, personally, truly create your own reality now.

Your new self-awareness, your view into the world may surprise even you. All good. Progress. Loving compassion for self and others in our world will take us everywhere we choose to go.

PART 3

Exploring the Inner Landscape of Your Creative and Imaginative Feeling Self

EXPLORATIONS 9–16

Continuing the Grand Tour:
On the Way to Your Heart

INTRODUCTION:
Sounding Out New Territory on the Way to Your Heart

I am here, always, as storyteller, and as your guide, while you delve a little into the inner layers of yourself

throughout these next Explorations. Take heart!

These are not at all as difficult as you might at first imagine.

We shall explore your self-care somewhat more thoroughly in this section. By searching your heartfelt feelings each time you approach the idea of doing something with the emotions which may arise, you will come closer to knowing your true self at a far deeper level. These Explorations need to be undertaken when you are calm and centered, not in a high state of emotional stress. Most likely, only in a level of your meditation state, or while practicing the breathing mentioned earlier, are you going to achieve deeper knowledge to make needed changes for your self-care.

Our journey together into the hinterland of yourself has brought you to the point of greater self-awareness. This state of being, of being more in charge of you, can be called sovereignty of self. You do understand yourself so much more than before you began this journey, and you have discovered that there is so much more to you than you had any idea of before this. Well done!

It has been said that we are here on Earth to learn how to use the energies available to us to grow into the self-knowledge that can bring us to be more fully human, in the best sense possible.

Having taken yourself through Explorations 1 through 8, your stance in the world is most likely one in which you are able to examine the world around you. You are more able to see how you may fit into this new world we find ourselves in, and you have probably learned how to use to your advantage your new self-care tool, Sounding Out Your Feelings.

Lately, we have come through some major world events, world-wide heat waves in summer, dangerous flooding, political upheavals, and other natural disasters throughout the globe. How has this state of affairs affected how you relate *to you*? During these next Explorations into your heartland, we shall be visiting places you perhaps rarely, if ever, visit. These places are not unknown to you; there are many views and landscapes of the mental and emotional kind which we might glimpse here as we make our way through your Feelings-Heartland.

Sometimes you may be delighted with what you find, but maybe not always. We shall not stay long there, as it could be somewhat difficult territory for you.

Know that you are always guided and loved as you explore these possibly unpleasant areas of self that you have been hiding. Do not become alarmed or saddened, since clearing these pathways can lead to a stronger, more loving heart. Do not attempt to plough through hard places if you become in dire need. Whenever the going gets rough, find someone to talk to, be it friend or professional help.

We may, too, touch on some pleasurable memories which can bring you joy and a lift to your spirits. These are just as necessary to your state of wellbeing as is the clearing out of old baggage. Remember, allow yourself to be comfortable with your emotions during this work. Cry, shout, rave, express your feelings. It is you that you are investigating, after all. Be kind to you.

Many a journey can have perilous events associated with it. These events are for humans to learn from and to grow. This you already know, and this prying into your inner being is not so hazardous as might seem at first glance. You are to be challenged, yes, but not to any extreme lengths. Just a little tipping of the emotional toe into those turbulent waters; nothing to fear but fear itself—often quoted, true in essence.

And who knows? You might even enjoy a quick look at some deeply moving events or emotions that bring a smile to your heart. Your emotions, as you now know, arise from your beliefs about you and your life. They are your treasures; we are just polishing them a little. In order to trigger one or several of your feelings in our exploring, let us delve into some situations that may bring up some remembrances of such events, often hidden, or pushed away or down in your own life. They may not fit your particular situation yet may have some resonance with it.

Do feel comfortable.

You have a strong guide at the head of this work,

I am still here, in my words, supporting you on this journey.

You will not be overcome if you stay calm and centered in yourself. Our goal is to discover what is in you that can be of great benefit to you as you make your way through this world. What makes you happy is key to your future. To be able to find joy is a great blessing.

Remember being on Terra and the knowledge you learned there? You can change what you do not like about yourself or your life—change your thoughts and beliefs. You might ask, "But will changing myself change how others in my life will react to me? Especially difficult people?" Yes, in large part, depending upon how you learn to be who you truly are with these people in your life. It is how you react to them and their behavior that determines your emotional responses.

We can remain here until you are sure enough to move beyond that Gateway.

Breathe easily and keep relaxed. Are you pleased or afraid, anticipating these next Explorations?

EXPLORATION 9:
Happy? Me?
I Guess I am, probably

Let us begin to explore the idea of your current state of happiness. In this kind of self-care, it is sometimes necessary to find where it hurts, and then to find a suitable and effective way to relieve this situation. Here we are using Sounding, with intention, to dig a little. Intentions come from this kind of searching of oneself. Be truly honest with yourself, if you can. When you hit a blockage and cannot move forward, take a break, a rest from the work. Let it all cook a bit.

If you are serious about making changes in your life and self, this work is worth the effort and the discomfort it may bring up for you. You are not hurting any other people. Your own happiness is on the line here. Of course, if any situation does occur that is of a medical nature, you must seek professional help. Sounding is self-care, not medical care.

So, how to go on in this search? With Sounding Out Your Feelings, of course.

Close your eyes and come with me

to the place just outside the Gateway to your mind,

and let us be here a little while to consider what we are about to do.

Bring yourself to your place of stillness.

Allow your body to be at ease.

Allow your breathing to be quiet and even.

Feel the direction of your breath as you bring it into your body—

through the nostrils, down your throat, and into your lungs.

Feel the breath as you gently breathe it out again through slightly parted lips.

For the next few breaths, be present, mindful of your breathing.

Watch any ideas and thoughts as they come in and take up space in your mind.

Just watch them as they leave, without taking up residence there.

Calmly and willingly let go of them.

With the exhalation of each breath, you notice how your body is beginning to feel more relaxed, your heart rate settles down, and tensions loosen.

You are coming into Quiet-mind.

Remain here during your Sounding.

Riding on your sound, begin Sounding Out Your Feelings,

and we will again approach the gateway to your inner being and your heart.

Do you see that there is yet one other keeper here who waits to greet you and is holding up a kind of curtain before you? Do you truly wish to discover what is behind this seemingly transparent curtain?

Take courage, friend, and step up to look into the eyes of this other you—yes, *you*.

At first you might find it difficult to look because for so long you have shielded yourself from truths about who you are and what makes you happy, or what you would like to make you happy, even if you have resolved many of your difficulties around this idea in the previous Explorations. Cheer up!

Here you might like to make the intention to find out more about what could make you happy and begin Sounding.

Come with me!

Imaginatively step around this curtain that is being held up to you. Look behind it.

What do you find there?

Once more, there is that beautiful garden appearing through the glass-like door.

Pause for a moment, while still Sounding, to enjoy the colors and shapes you perceive here.

Let your imagination bring you down that pathway which is opening up

as you gaze beyond that other guardian self.

Let us take a few steps along this way.

You notice now how light begins to show you more of the way ahead.

You see a small pond with tall grasses swaying around its edges.

Go and sit near this pond.

We have some thinking to do.

Let us consider *how you know yourself today*. "What a statement," you may think.

How do you recognize your happiness state?

Is it due to how safe you feel?

Or how much money you have to live on

comfortably?

Do you like your home?

How about those you live with; are they compatible or not?

Are you living alone? If so, what is that like for you?

How do you feel about the work you do to earn your living?

You may want to explore all of these questions and more for yourself and find the truth within. Real truth, deeply felt. We are delving into feelings and emotions to find your true self. Self-care is the name of this game we are playing, remember.

Here are some more ideas for you to consider:
- So, maybe you are a plodder; you just get where you need to go?
- Are you a well-rounded scholar?
- Do you dislike going to classes?
- Are you an artist who loves working with colors and shapes?
- You did not enjoy geometry in school?
- You were, however, good at math and science?
- You love to use your hands to make things?
- Do you enjoy reading to gain knowledge?

- Do you enjoy relaxing in front of your screen?
- Does your partner add much to your enjoyment of life so that you do not have a lot to do to sustain yourself?
- Do you live alone and wish to have a partner—or not?

These are some important ways to look at YOU. There are many other ways to see yourself.

How do I know? I have been somewhere along such paths as these, too.

Much more is to be experienced in this world: Do you long for something more to make you truly happy?

Have you made your intention yet?

Hold this intention in some part of your awareness and let us continue to make sound.

Deepen your breathing, and begin to allow your sounds to arise within you.

As you are Sounding Out Your Feelings,

observe images, or pictures, or objects, or feelings that come in.

Let your sounds soar as you explore your feelings about what can make you happy.

Stay with the sounds until you know it is the natural stopping point, and go into the silence,

still in your Quiet-mind, and let these sounds do their healing work.

Solutions may suggest themselves to you in this silence.

When you are ready, inhale and exhale, open your eyes, and stretch.

Bring your outer senses back online.

You are back in your everyday world.

Thinking of making some changes in your life after this Sounding? Large or small? Your intention will, naturally, bring about some things that change in your life, and you have the courage now to go ahead with what you feel impulsed to do to get the changes happening.

Good work!

EXPLORATION 10:
Abandoned? Left Out of the Picture?

Here I will tell a tale that may have some resonance with you and your own experiences. This telling may make your heart feel a little better protected from any deep, puzzling hurt that may arise during this next excursion into your Heartland. Otherwise, enjoy exploring.

My tale begins with two high-school girls who were good friends, Ellie and Lina. Ellie had begun seeing an older boy from their school, who was generally regarded as being fast, a Don Juan of the town. Without her telling Lina about this, Lina was later to hear of this from others. She felt left out. That went deep. However, the other more deeply felt shock was felt when Lina was called to the office of the Reverend Mother, Head of School.

Her dear friend Ellie had made a sudden decision to join the convent, the Reverend Mother told her. And would she, Lina, also consider joining the nuns as her dear friend had done?

Such a thought had never entered Lina's mind. She was also reeling from the shock and hurt that Ellie had not confided in her. No, she told the nun, she had other plans for her life out in the world!

As the years went by and Lina became more aware of this world, she realized that this Romeo might have gone a little bit far with innocent Ellie, and frightened her to go scampering into the arms of the Sisters for refuge from sin and sex. She had, most likely, been hustled away by her teachers to the Novitiate School of their Mother House of the Order. Ellie probably had not had an opportunity to speak to Lina. Perhaps, she could have contacted her later, if permitted? Nevertheless, this small betrayal of friendship had run deep in Lina all those years unexplored, until she found a possible reason for Ellie's behavior. Lina never heard any more of her erstwhile friend.

This vignette allows for some redemption for the girl Lina who found excuses for her friend Ellie, easing her heart somewhat, with a sense of forgiveness.

Time seems irrelevant in such cases because, actually, time itself is an illusion for those who live on Earth.

So you, too, may discover within yourself a similar kind of abandonment or betrayal. Only you may recognize its cause, because you now have tools to do so.

Form your intention, if and when you find yourself in a similar situation, and let us go adventuring!

Close your eyes,

and come with me

to that place just outside

the entranceway to your mind and heart,

and let us be here a while to consider what we are about to do.

Allow your body to be at ease.

Allow your breathing to be quiet and even.

Feel the direction of your breath as you bring it into your body—

through your nostrils, down your throat, and into your lungs.

Feel the breath as you gently breathe it out again, through slightly parted lips.

For the next few breaths, be present, mindful of your breathing.

Watch any ideas or thoughts as they come in and take up space in your mind.

Just watch them as they leave, without taking up residence there.

Calmly and willingly let go of them.

With the exhalation of each breath, you notice now how

your body is beginning to feel more at ease,

your heart rate settles down, and tensions loosen.

You are coming into Quiet-mind.

Remain here as you go Sounding.

Begin your sounds, while keeping your intention in some part of your awareness

and allow those sounds to soar as you are Sounding Out Your Feelings.

Continue Sounding while we contemplate entering through our imaginary Gateway

to the garden of your inner self once again.

Do you see, over to your left, a tall maple tree in full new leaf?

A wooden bench at its base is just the thing for us to take a short rest here.

Come with me!

Send your sounds into the mass of green leaves and let us sit here to consider where

you would like to go from here on this

Exploration into your heartland.

Feel the coolness of sitting beneath these huge leafy branches.

Look up and feel a soft breeze as it goes by, touching your face.

See ahead of you through the leaves of some low-hanging branches.

Do you observe a figure coming towards you through the dappling sunlight?

Their features are becoming clear to you, and you recognize this person.

Ah, yes—an old friend from your past. A hesitant smile lingers on this face,

not quite sure of how you might feel about them.

Gesture to this person to come and sit next to you.

What do you feel? Be honest. It is fine to have these feelings.

That is what these Explorations are all about.

Are you angry? Or sad? Or pleased?

Bring your feelings closer and examine them,

just enough to align with your intention.

Any deeper look might become enough for you to go and get help!

Can you acknowledge who this person is and what they have meant to

you in the past? Is it easy enough to dialogue with them?

Are you coming to a place of some reconciliation with this one?

Continue Sounding Out Your Feelings,

and, as you are able, release any feelings that arise from your feeling center.

When you come to the natural silence and stillness after the sounds,

be still in Quiet-mind and remain here,

as the sounds do their work in you and the cells of your body,

bringing you into a better place of well-being in body, mind, soul, and heart.

When you are ready,

inhale and exhale, open your eyes, and stretch.

Bring your outer senses back online.

You are back in your everyday world.

EXPLORATION 11:
Heavenly Scent, or Not?

Many roads must be traveled during a lifetime, and so it is for you. Yet here we simply walk amongst the pathways to your inner feelings, to your heartland. We find gentle sloping paths that may go deep into you,or may just be short interludes into the layers of the inner feeling self. This depends upon you and your willingness to upturn events from your past.

You know yourself well by this time.

You are being asked, or challenged, throughout these Explorations to truly examine the depths of your feelings about your life, not about others, but about you affecting your life.

By what? By your beliefs about this life you are living.

Try making a list of ideas you have regarding who you currently think you are and what you are. If this is too difficult, then perhaps these next few Explorations can give you clues to those beliefs or attitudes you hold about who or what you think you are in this world, beliefs which you haven't yet considered during your

sojourn through these Explorations so far.
>You may be in for a surprise.

>With your eyes closed,
>
>come with me
>
>to the place just outside the entranceway
>
>to your mind and heart,
>
>and let us be here a little while to consider what we are about to do.

>Allow your body to be at ease.
>
>Allow your breathing to be quiet and easy.
>
>Feel the direction of your breath as you bring it into your body—
>
>through the nostrils, down your throat, and into your lungs.
>
>Feel the breath gently going out again, through slightly parted lips.
>
>For the next few breaths, be present, mindful of your breathing.
>
>Watch any ideas and thoughts coming in and taking up space in your awareness.
>
>Just watch them as they leave, without taking up residence there.

Calmly and willingly let go of them.

With the exhalation of each breath,

you notice how your body is beginning to feel more at ease.

Your heart rate settles down, and tensions loosen.

You are coming into Quiet-mind and Heart.

Begin Sounding, and hold your intention in some part of your mind.

As you enter through the Gateway, what can you smell, imaginatively?

Roses? Lavender? Eucalyptus? Wet soil?

It may be a smell or perfume you enjoy.

Also though, it could be a scent you despise.

Think about this: Is it causing you enjoyment or irritation?

Examine what you feel, and see if you get a sense of where

the feeling comes from. An event? Or favorite plant?

Bring this idea of what causes this feeling to the surface of your mind.

Take a long look, because it holds a key to your

hidden emotion that

now needs to come up for you to examine and to possibly release.

This is not meant to be a difficult act,

but one that is simply for you to take a look at from this moment

in your present time, and not in that darker past that haunted you.

The pleasant scent of flowers is truly a gift that can bring a pleasant,

enjoyable time from your memory that is much more beneficial to you.

The imaginative garden path we are traveling together forms part of your memories related to some of those perfumes and scents you remember. Was it something you were wearing when you were in that experience that opened your heart to love? Who did you love? Was it deeply, or just a teenage crush? Such experiences mature us, and how we cope with them can leave a lasting pattern on our emotional body.

Look harder at this situation you have isolated. Was it reciprocated or simply the young crush from afar? Answer as truly as you remember, and allow some of those feelings to emerge as you focus on them during your Sounding. Your young heart, if indeed it was hurt, is clearing much of those hurtful, unreciprocated feelings, or hurts that loving another brought to you, while you are Sounding Out Your Feelings.

Besides any real and deeply felt pleasure, from that association with another who reciprocated your love, is a forgotten joy embedded in this memory, and yet some residual hurts may still be in your heart.

Your intention will act to support those memories of the 'love that got away' with a sense of neutrality towards that person. Whenever, in your future, you come across that scent or perfume, any old emotional ties will not have such pulls on your emotions to upset or remind you of that old love. It is not necessary or healthy to hold fast to old hurts, not at all.

The idea of forgiveness would work well here. And perhaps a little pleasure?

Those hurts leave easily and fast during the Sounding, if you truly desire that they no longer have any meaning or influence over you. Think of the lessons you have learned from such experiences, and you can smile at such remembrances.

> Let your breath deepen your Quiet-mind
>
> and allow your Sounding to arise from deep in your heart.

Stay with this for as long as you deem it necessary to bring you

to a more comfortable place.

Then go into the silence to allow for the cells of your body and heart to be eased.

When you are ready, inhale and exhale, open your eyes, and stretch.

Bring your outer senses back online.

You are back in your everyday world.

Remember any thoughts, ideas, colors or shapes that came in during your Sounding and in the silence. All such clues help you to recognize how you are coming into a better place in well-being in body, mind, and heart.

EXPLORATION 12:
The Pitter-Patter of Iron-Clad Boots

Do you remember the first moment when you realized that your parents or guardians were not the infallible beings you had, until then, perceived them to be? If so, at what age did this happen? Were you pre-teen or a little older? The first stage of this recognition may occur when maturing into an adult begins. It can feel painful, or it can be a great release, a sense of freedom to your growing awareness of self.

In Exploration 12 we shall look at a short vignette that may evoke in you some related experience that could benefit from a little exploring into the emotional content of your own experience.

As children we are vulnerable to the whims and decisions of those who are our most closely watched and often revered adults, or near adults. Sometimes it may be another family member, or friend of the family. These are our heroes as young children on our way to being grown-up. They are not always as heroic as we perceived them to be then. They too may be as vulnerable to the whims and expectations of the world around them.

Have you identified your own experience of this kind?

If so, make your intention here.

Vignette: One day a student of mine came to tell me, excited in the telling, that his parents had decided to move to another state. He looked so happy with all of his newly developed plans for his future, until a day or so later. His parents, on second thoughts, reneged on their original decision. The boy was cast into deep, dark disappointment. He felt angry with them for not going forward with their decision to move, and also for telling him too soon before they had properly thought this through. For him, in the new place, many opportunities had beckoned.

Although they did not tell him their reasons for backing out of the decision to move, he still felt strong resentment towards his parents. He allowed these emotions and feelings to color much of his growing-up years, and they affected decisions he made during this time.

With Sounding, he came, much later, to understand this situation more fully and was able to release some of his resentment and anger.

We carry forward so much from our younger years without fully understanding the underlying causes of situations that trigger our responses. We hold resentment towards those who were our mentors when young, without realizing that this colors our relationships with these people.

Using Sounding as a tool for self-care to, at least, bring up much of those feelings can be beneficial to your sense of well-being.

Search your heart; look into the corners, in the folds of your inner being, to clear any of this kind of suppressed feeling you may discover there.

> Be in the moment with your breath,
>
> Close your eyes and come with me to the place
>
> just outside the entranceway to your mind and heart.
>
> Let us be here a while to consider what we are about to do.
>
> Allow your body to be at ease.
>
> Allow your breathing to be quiet and even.
>
> Feel the direction of your breath as you bring it into your body—
>
> through the nostrils, down your relaxed throat, and into your lungs.

Feel the breath as you gently breathe it out again through slightly parted lips.

For the next few breaths, be present, mindful of your breathing.

Watch any ideas and thoughts as they come in and take up space in your mind,

just watch them as they leave, without taking up residence there.

Calmly and willingly let go of them.

With the exhalation of each breath, you notice how your body is beginning

to feel more at ease. Your heart rate settles down, and tensions loosen.

You are coming into Quiet-mind.

Remain here during your Sounding, which you can begin now.

Let us go, imaginatively, down to the Gateway once more to gaze about you.

There is a human shadow just beyond that archway we have seen before.

Come! Let us go over and see who it is.

Is it one of your parents or your guardian?

Or is it someone else who in your youth had a

strong influence over you?

Call them by name to come out of the shadow to speak to you.

Do you want an apology or something else?

You are in control of this situation now, so speak up.

Say your piece and let this one know the damage caused

by their behavior towards you when you were young.

Allow your sounds to arise from within your body and,

keeping your intention in some part of your awareness,

sound out your feelings.

When you come to the natural silence, be still and be aware of

any thoughts, colors, shapes, feelings that come to your awareness.

These are keys to how you have released at least some of your feelings

regarding this matter. Remember how your body feels.

When you are ready, inhale and exhale, open your eyes, and stretch.

Bring your outer senses back online.

You are back in your everyday world.

Were you able to come to some kind of resolution with this person? Do you still hold bad feelings against this one? You may, at some later stage, want to do another Sounding in regard to this matter.

EXPLORATION 13:
Lucky Thirteen?

"If you want to know the secrets of the Universe think: energy, vibration, and frequency."

—Nikola Tesla

Do you consider 13 to be your lucky number, even feeling a little foolish to admit it? Numbers are important clues to the structures of the Universe, as many scientists will attest.

So, not so silly, especially when you imbue your chosen number, or group of numbers, with the energy of your beliefs around this idea of good luck, or bad luck. This is a game, although a rather serious one you are playing with the Universe. It can be most powerful in manifesting for you. But you cannot manifest for others—we cannot interfere with the life path of another person.

Mathematics are expressed throughout the Universe, as in the many and various layers of consciousness, dimensions, and in the relationships of the planets and stars to each other in space. Read Einstein's theory of relativity and later works. Look at the Mandelbrot set of fractal theory. Astrophysicists explore the Universe with highly developed mathematical formulae to make discoveries throughout the Universe, and through the use of these formulae, discover new stars or planets, or asteroids.

Yes, numbers are important. The human body is estimated to have about forty trillion cells all working in amazing harmony to create our bodies. How lucky is that?

Are you one of the lucky people who see repeating sets of numbers, usually in threes? Often these series may appear on registration plates on automobiles, but they can show up anywhere for you to see them. For some there are specific meanings for each group. However, you may arrive at your own set of interpretations. Books have been written on this subject. These sets are nudges for you to pay attention to your reality. Some people get nudges in other ways: music, song lyrics, repeated phrases, for instance. These symbols are coming to you from your Inner Self to guide you to be alert to something in your life that needs fixing or expanding in some way. Maybe, your lucky number will change now that you have a different perspective on numbers.

Have fun with them!

Make your intention to get clearer messages from your inner self, or compose your own intention.

Be in the present moment with your breath.

Close your eyes and come with me to the place just outside the entranceway to your mind and heart,

and let us be here a while to consider what we are about to do.

Allow your body to be at ease.

Allow your breathing to be quiet and even.

Feel the direction of your breath as you bring it into your body—

through the nostrils, down your throat, and into your lungs.

Feel the breath as you gently breathe it out again through slightly parted lips.

For the next few breaths, be present, mindful of your breathing.

Watch any ideas and thoughts as they come in and take up space in your mind.

Just watch them as they leave, without taking up residence there.

Calmly, willingly let go of them.

SOUNDING OUT YOUR FEELINGS

With the exhalation of each breath, you notice how your body

is beginning to feel more at ease. Your heart rate is settling down

and tensions loosen.

You are coming into Quiet-mind.

Remain here as you begin your Sounding.

On the wings of your sounds,

let those sounds arise from within your body.

Exult in the richness of your voice as

you are Sounding Out Your Feelings

to help you discover some of the meanings of

the groups of numbers which appear in your reality.

When you come to the natural silence, be still here and watch for ideas or thoughts.

These may be your clues to understanding those numbers.

When you are ready, inhale and exhale, open your eyes, stretch.

Bring your outer senses back online.

You are back in your everyday world.

EXPLORATION 14:
Grace Comes in the Morning

Are you aware that you have been holding a grudge against someone for a while, be it someone you know, or even a well-known personality, a politician, or a media person? A grudge is a feeling of blame or dislike towards another for some action that you perceived this person had perpetrated, not necessarily against you, but just as a probable action. It is a belief, of course, and one that does not serve to bring you pleasure, but one that aggravates your sense of right or wrong. It does you no good at all.

Look into your memory banks and see if you find any such thought or feeling, however small or innocuous it seems.

In this Exploration we are allowing this kind of odd belief to be unearthed for the sake of your comfort and happiness, or as a reflection of some later, bigger grudge that may occur. A reminder.

Here is a story from an old friend, unearthed during a Sounding session with me. She admitted it to me almost like a confession, and at least, her telling of it was cathartic for her.

My friend had a favorite ring, set with diamonds and sapphires, which she thought she had put away safely out of reach of children and others visiting her home. When it occurred one day that she wanted to wear it to an upcoming event, she went looking for it where she expected she had put it sometime previously. It was not there! Immediately she had the idea that her cleaning person had put it somewhere else. Then, she began to blame this poor woman as if she had stolen the ring. With her mind set on blaming another person, she endeavored to put the incident out of her mind.

When my friend shared this story, she smiled sheepishly and told me she had recently, after so many years, found the ring where it had been securely hidden. For so long she had held this idea of blame towards another person in her emotional body. Only when it came to the surface during a Sounding Out Your Feelings session with me, did she unearth her hidden feelings.

A grudge held for so long in the emotional body can act like a sore that will not heal. A small thing, and seemingly forgotten. Yet it does color some of your thinking in ways you do not realize. When you dig a little into the feeling center, your Heart Space, you may be surprised to find a grudge there. If this is so, this Exploration and sounding can be of some help to you to shift the feelings to a more comfortable place or dispel the grudge altogether.

And here is a good place to form an intention to do so.

> Close your eyes and come with me
>
> to the entranceway to your mind and heart,
>
> and let us be here a little while to consider what we are about to do.
>
> Allow your body to be at ease.
>
> Allow your breathing to be quiet and even.
>
> Feel the direction of your breath as you bring it into your body—
>
> through the nostrils, down your throat, and into your lungs.
>
> Feel the breath as you gently breathe it out again through slightly parted lips.
>
> For the next few breaths, be present, mindful of your breathing.
>
> Watch any ideas and thoughts as they come in and take up space in your mind.
>
> Just watch them as they leave, without taking up residence there.

Calmly and willingly let go of them.

With the exhalation of each breath, you notice now how your body is beginning

to feel more at ease. Your heart rate settles down and tensions loosen.

You are coming into Quiet-mind.

With your intention in some part of your awareness,

Allow your sounds to arise from deep in your body,

and on the wings of those sounds,

begin to Sound Out Your Feelings

to eliminate any grudges you may have discovered.

Come to the natural silence, remaining in Quiet-mind,

and be here for a while to let the sounds do their work of healing your body and heart.

When you are ready, inhale and exhale, open your eyes, and stretch.

Bring your outer senses back online.

You are back in your everyday world.

EXPLORATION 15:
Happy Days

Being in a relationship with someone or something for some years is a long-term job.

Many people who are in such a situation with another may find joy, comfort, and a sense of security. Others may find the opposite, or something like half and half. Are you in such a partnership? Let us take a brief look, to find out if you want or need changes there, and how you might go about bringing possible change into your reality.

Do you need more private time to yourself?

Are you always at the beck and call of the other person, or partner, who is needy and wants your attention? Or do you perform this helpful role, expecting your partner to take an active role in your welfare?

Be clear and transparent with yourself if you can.

How does this relationship fulfill your needs and wants as a person?

How do you succeed in being who you want to be without leaving the other person unfulfilled and lonely?

These and other questions do need your frank answers so that you can move on in your life to become more adult, more fully human, and to grow spiritually, psychologically, and emotionally.

Are you being a mirror for that person's personality traits, even likes and dislikes? Or do you see, reflected back to you from your partner, your own personality traits? Examine your own behavior to find out if you are acting in these ways, not being your own sovereign self. Once you have considered your position in the relationship, reconsider your intention here to help rectify any of these behaviors that you find incompatible with who you are now becoming.

> Close your eyes,
>
> and come with me to the place just outside the entranceway
>
> to your mind and heart,
>
> and let us be here awhile to consider what we are about to do.
>
> Allow your body to be at ease.
>
> Allow your breathing to be quiet and even.
>
> Feel the direction of your breath as you bring it into your body—

through the nostrils, down your throat, and into your lungs.

Feel the breath as you gently breathe it out again through slightly parted lips.

For the next few breaths, be present, mindful of your breathing

as you watch any ideas and thoughts as they come in and take up space in your mind.

Just watch them as they leave without taking up residence there.

Calmly and willingly let go of them.

With the exhalation of each breath, you notice now how your body is

beginning to feel more at ease. Your heart rate settles down.

Tensions loosen. You are coming into Quiet-mind.

Remain here, and begin your Sounding.

Walk with me through the Gateway, in your imagination,

and let us go together along one of the paths leading away from the Gateway.

We are coming to a place you know well—it is your own kitchen!

Is there anyone here that you recognize? Ah, yes—your partner, waiting to have a talk with you.

What is the subject that comes up first? Is it that you do not do your share of the housework?

Who does most of the cooking? Do you spend a lot of quality time together? Do you share many interests, such as music, film, authors, dance, or sports?

These are some important building blocks for a strong relationship. Feel what your partner might say to you about one or two of these subjects, or of any you can name for yourself. Do you share spiritual or religious beliefs? Do you have an agreement about how you both see your relationship faring from this point onward? Observe your feelings here. Be realistic, but always kind and loving.

Have you formed your intention, yet?

Keep this intention in some part of your awareness during this Exploration into your relationship.

And now allow your sounds to arise from deep in your body and heart.

Continue until you come to the natural silence,

remaining in Quiet-mind.

Be still here to let your sounds work their magic on you and your heart.

When you are ready, inhale and exhale, open your eyes, stretch, and breathe.

Bring your outer senses back online.

You are back in your everyday world.

EXPLORATION 16:
Pets Passing—Waiting for them to go

Pets can be as important to their families as can humans. Pets are often given the position of loved members of the family. I, and several of my friends, have had our pets pass after long illnesses. The waiting and the watching become an agony. Well-meaning vets advise pet owners to keep them comfortable. So, this we lovingly do, with breaking hearts, knowing the end could come any day. When the pet does pass, without assistance, a great and shocking sadness envelops their families. If it is required that the poor animal is in such distress that they are taken to a vet to be 'put down,' that very act is taken on by some of the family members who may feel as if they had 'killed' their beloved animal themselves, feeling the awfulness of that responsibility. This emotional shock may last for a long time; it is truly like a human family member dying.

Mourning can be debilitating and even lead to mental/emotional illnesses. Grief counseling is often helpful. A natural death is, in some ways, easier to cope with, as family and friends help. Sadness and mourning can still take an emotional toll. Here we use Sounding to help alleviate some of the pain. It may be of some comfort to know that each of us human, animal, insect, indeed, all life, has a lifespan that is often called the life path. Our pets, too, have a life path. This is not the same as predestination. So, feeling guilty of assisting these loving creatures to leave this Earthly life is not a true perspective at all. Helping them to leave when their time is up is an act of love towards them. Perhaps they have lost the strength, through debilitating illness, to make the final effort.

Whatever the case, your pet appreciates your loving kindness and responds with love. It has been said that pets are of the Angelic Realm, though not angels themselves, and love us unconditionally. Most of us have, at some time, had to experience the passing of a friend or a beloved person or a pet. Perhaps you are waiting and watching for a relative or a friend or a beloved pet to pass over.

During this Sounding session, have the intention that you will receive some comforting acknowledgement of your feelings for your pet.

> Close your eyes and come with me
> to the place just outside the entranceway to your

mind and heart,

and let us be here a little while to consider what we are about to do.

Allow your body to be at ease.

Allow your breathing to be quiet and even.

Feel the direction of your breath as you bring it into your body—

through the nostrils, your throat, and down into your lungs.

Feel the breath as you gently breathe it out again through slightly parted lips.

For the next few breaths, be present, mindful of your breathing.

Watch any ideas and thoughts as they come in and take up space in your mind.

Just watch them as they leave without taking up residence there.

Calmly and willingly let go of them.

With the exhalation of each breath, you notice now how your body is

beginning to feel more at ease. Your heart rate settles down and tensions loosen.

You are coming into Quiet-mind.

Remain here during your Sounding.

Begin to allow your sounds to arise from within your body and heart.

We are once again imaginatively at the Gateway to your mind and heart.

Open the Gateway. Let it swing back behind you. You know the way out.

We will follow that old grassy path towards a small, green-hedged enclosure.

Do you hear the sounds of happy play amongst some puppies?

Why not go over there and discover what it is all about?

Here is your own beloved pet standing up to greet you with joyful yelps and jumps!

You move closer and caress your pet. Such loving feelings come over you.

Your pet seems fully alive and well!

It is so, because all of those pets in the enclosure are in spirit form.

In truth, your pets are never far from your own energy field.

Continue with your Sounding, until you come to the natural silence,

still in your Quiet-mind, and be here comfortably until you sense a healing

of your heart in regard to your intention.

When you are ready, inhale and exhale, open your eyes, and stretch.

Bring your outer senses back online.

You are back in your everyday world.

PART 4

Exploring the Inner Landscape of Your Creative, Imaginative, Inner Feeling Self

EXPLORATIONS 17 – 20

On the Rocky Road to Your Inner Self

Up until this point in our Explorations together, we have been concentrating on your approach to the outer world you live in and to how that world responds to you. As we made our journey through these Explorations, I shared some of my own secrets to well-being. For the Explorations to come, I shall assist you in finding ways to open up within you avenues to some of the secrets to be found there, in your inner self: that deep part of you that is connected to other areas of you that are not part of this three-dimensional, physical world.

Having read and worked this far in, you may have changed a great deal. Now I will offer some rather unusual Explorations for you to try. Go easy with these if you are new to this kind of information. It is meant as self-care.

Let's have some fun and go adventuring!

When you let go of so much untruth regarding who and what you are in this lifetime, you can easily insert new ideas or beliefs about yourself, as you have been doing throughout the Explorations that you have decided to explore.

It is to be hoped that you are in a happy and contented place right now so that you can enjoy these next excursions into the inner-dimensional world. You may already have a grasp of this kind of inner experience.

Let us take a look at some of the ways you interact with your inner being and other realms of existence: dreams, visions, angelic interventions, knowings, imagination, and other fun experiences. This is to be a teaching about deeper, inner-self work that uses sound and intention to go into the areas of you that have seemed to be hidden from you. Yet you do know something of this self. It governs what you think and do, including your hidden beliefs—those lurking ideas that you tend to ignore and cover over with that everyday 'self-talk. And yet there is far more to this inner self, as I hope you will discover during this extraordinary romp through consciousness with me.

You are worthy. You are loved and honored. You are here to learn more about yourself and your abilities as a human being, because Earth is a school where we may find our way through the density of three-dimensional fog and noise, if you have the courage to come with me!

So many of our explorations in this part will be examining your beliefs regarding your Soul Path. No easy passes here. But go lightly. This work is for those who are dedicated to growing their souls or to obtaining an awareness of higher consciousness.

This ability grows with practice, as do most rewarding efforts in earthly life, and with knowledge. The school of hard knocks? In a way. But far more rewarding. And it can be fun!

You can look yourself in the eye because you are aware that you are a spiritual being in physical form, learning more about how to be in the body and to grow your soul. Far-fetched? No! However, because of this situation of physical form in a physical world, you have been taught so much that goes against the concept of your having a soul and of being a spiritual being as well as having a mind and a body.

We will look at some short stories, vignettes, some from my own experiences, to show you something of how your inner world works with you to help you to progress on your Soul Path.

EXPLORATION 17:
Guardian Angels

Have you ever noticed that sometimes in dangerous situations where people are hurt, someone comes forward to give needed assistance and then cannot be located to receive gratitude?

Who are these good Samaritans, you may wonder? They are here to make sure you continue to live your life through to the end of your lifespan. As humans we are prone to making bad decisions that may lead to accidents that threaten our lives. Since we agree to be here to learn life lessons, such accidents could cause us to leave here too soon, before those lessons are encountered or completed by us. So our guides, or guardian angels, or Earth angels may step in. It is their business to see us keep going. I will tell you of two instances when my own life was challenged by my lack of knowledge that might have prevented such events.

I might have been four years old. My family and I were visiting my aunt in another town, one I did not know.

We were taken to the local swimming pool. This was something new to me, at that age. I had never before seen people swimming in a large tub of water. I was used to the ocean and the gentle waves at the seashore washing round my ankles. No deeper.

So, with one foot on the edge of the pool, the other dipping in and out of the shallow waters of the pool, I began to move along the perimeter of this big tub, intending to progress around the whole thing. The water began to get higher around my ankle each step I took, but not so much to alarm me at all. Soon, to my surprise, because I did not know it could happen, I was toppling over into the deeper end of the pool. I could see, with my eyes open under the water, bubbles through the water as I went down to the hard pool floor. I felt myself rising to the surface for the third time, in a strange state of disordered thinking. Suddenly, someone was jumping into the water near me, coming close enough to grab my arm. I felt myself being pulled through the water and dumped onto the grass beside the pool.

This person, a big boy I thought, then steered me towards my mother and my aunt. They cuddled me, then looked up to thank the boy. He was gone. No one had seen him. The boy was not seen again, and no one at the pool had known him, nor had not even noticed him being there. He simply melded into the crowd. Definitely some kind of angel.

We get help or assistance throughout our lives from these beings from another level of existence. They abound amongst us, ready to assist us with keeping us on our life path. Have you had a similar experience or something like? If so, make an intention here to be grateful that you are alive and to ask for help any time you need it in future.

> Close your eyes and come with me
>
> to the place just outside the entranceway to your mind and heart,
>
> and let us be here a little while
>
> to consider what we are about to do.
>
> Allow your body to be at ease.
>
> Allow your breathing to be quiet and even.
>
> Feel the direction of your breath as you bring it into your body—
>
> through the nostrils, down your throat, and into your lungs.
>
> Feel the breath as you breathe it gently out again through slightly parted lips.

For the next few breaths, be present and mindful of your breathing.

Watch any ideas or thoughts as they come in and take up space in your mind.

Just watch them as they leave, without taking up residence there.

Calmly and willingly let them go.

With the exhalation of each breath, you notice now how your body is beginning to feel more at ease.

Your heart rate settles down. Tensions loosen.

You are coming into Quiet-mind.

Remain here during your Sounding.

With your intention in some part of your awareness,

Bring your sounds to fullness and begin

Sounding Out Your Feelings.

When you come to the natural silence, stay in Quiet-mind

to allow your sounds to work on the cells and your energy fields.

This state of mind will bring you to some resolution of how you responded to the remembrance of such an episode in your life that resonates with that of mine from the above vignette.

When you are ready, inhale and exhale, open your eyes, and stretch.

Bring your outer senses back online.

You are back in your everyday world.

EXPLORATION 18:
Earth Angels

There exist some good people who, prompted by the goodness of their hearts, go into dangerous situations to help others. It seems as if promptings come from out of nowhere to those observing.

There are beings on Earth whose job it is to go into, say, that burning building or that horrible car crash, and rescue someone or stay with them until help arrives. You may already have heard such stories. Not all are courageous firefighters, it seems. Yet it is the same kind of energy that activates your guardian to intervene for you.

This comes from your inner self that guides and helps you manifest the life you are living, all based on what you believe about yourself and your life. Beliefs again? Yes. These ideas govern your life, because your emotions arise as a result of what you believe, and so you act from these emotions.

Luckily you are aware now of many of your own beliefs that have been governing your life to date.

Changing them if you do not want or like or need them anymore can be as easy as changing your coat. Once you identify an unhelpful belief and have examined it, assessed its current use to you, and found it a limiting one, you then think of a better replacement and adopt it, letting the old one go. Easy! Using Sounding to help change the vibration of the old belief is quick and effective, as you now are aware.

Having trouble accepting the idea of Earth Angels and Guardian Angels?

Here is another short story, a vignette, again from my own life experience, that illustrates this kind of intervention.

Vignette: Beware the Undertow!

We went to the West Beach on a sunny summer day, my sister and I. It was the Christmas holidays, (this was in Tasmania, that upside-down place in the Southern Hemisphere). I was almost eleven years old, and my sister Jan was fourteen.

Jan mildly flirted with a group of lifeguards, while I decided to go into the ocean for a paddle at the edge of the waves. I went a little farther than was safe for me, and suddenly the strong surf swept me off my feet and carried me out to sea. The bay was huge. Not being a strong swimmer, I was flotsam on the strong undertow.

Soon I was being carried out by the undertow way beyond where waves were little white caps dashing on to the sandy shore. I felt myself floating on the top of the strongly moving sea. My chances of getting back to shore seemed faint. I made an agreement with God: "If you let me live, and not drown, I will dedicate my life to being a good person." Something like that.

A long time, it seemed, after this conversation, one-sided as it was, I continued to float further out beyond the old stone breakwater wall. Helpless, and spitting out the salt water, I saw Denis, a neighbor, swimming some distance away from me. I called out to him to help me. He swam closer, recognizing me. He really did not believe me that I was in a helpless situation, thinking, I supposed then, that I was flirting with him. I did not flirt at my age of eleven! I was annoyed with him and told him so. Somehow, at last, I did convince him that I was a poor swimmer and needed help. He said he would go back to shore and get help. The waves were getting stronger. I had trouble staying up with my head out of the water. I grew tired.

I don't remember how long it was before I became aware of swimmers near to me. I felt my arms being taken in a firm grasp, propelling me towards the shore. Perhaps I blacked out. I remember only being stood up on my feet onto firm sand, and my sister standing over me with a cross face. It was not the joyful reception I had hoped for.

She had stopped keeping an eye on me to flirt with the boys from school. Now she stood waiting anxiously on the sand as my saviors brought me out of the water. She took control of me. I could not see the rescuers. They were not anywhere nearby. They had vanished. They were not known to my sister's friends, the regular Lifeguards.

Now I know that they were Earth angels who kept me alive. My exit point on my life-path was not to be then. So they stepped in. (The agreement I made with that higher power I have attempted to keep to this day as best I can.) Have you remembered a similar situation in your own life? If so, make your intention here for your own reasons. If this Exploration does not resonate with you, or with any of the other Explorations, simply go to the next one that does.

> Close your eyes and come with me
>
> to the place just outside the entranceway
>
> to your mind and heart, and let us be here a little while
>
> to consider what we are about to do.
>
> Allow your body to be at ease.
>
> Allow your breathing to be quiet and even.

Feel the direction of your breath as you bring it into your body—

through the nostrils, down your throat, and into the lungs.

Feel the breath as you gently breathe it out again through slightly parted lips.

For the next few breaths, be present and mindful of your breathing.

Watch any ideas or thoughts as they come in and take up space in your mind.

Just watch them as they leave without taking up residence there.

Calmly and willingly let go of them. With the exhalation of each breath, you notice

now how your body is beginning to feel more at ease.

Your heart rate settles down. Tensions loosen.

You are coming into Quiet-mind.

Remain here while you are Sounding.

Riding on your sounds, allow their vibrations to support your intention

to bring about some of those changes you would like to have in your life right now about how you perceive helpers from other realms of existence,

be they angelic beings or extra-terrestrial beings.

As you come to the natural silence, rest here in Quiet-mind, and let any images or thoughts come into your awareness as you feel the energies of the sounds make changes in you.

When you are ready, inhale and exhale, open your eyes, and stretch.

Bring your outer senses back online.

You are back in your everyday world.

EXPLORATION 19:
Death Singing

In some cultures, people have been known to make sounds like chanting when in the presence of one who is dying. Such rituals are meant to ease the leaving soul's way to its next life.

These days it is not usually part of the way we approach the dying process, which, more often than not, takes place in a hospital room or hospice setting, and is monitored by nursing staff. This practice would perhaps not be encouraged. Although there have been groups formed to allow instruments like harps played in the death room to create a calming atmosphere. In a more spiritual impulse, this may be a link to the old rituals.

Vignette: My own story illustrates this.

The story I relate to you is one that is deeply meaningful to me. It is about my dearest cousin who lay dying in hospital after a massive stroke. My niece called me in New York from Australia to tell me the shocking news. My cousin had always been the rock of the family. How could she be dying? I was engulfed in sobbing tears when my niece asked me to say something over the phone to my cousin who was unable to speak. I hesitated, wondering what to say.

My niece said, "Well, sing to her!"

My cousin and I had been professional classical singers, and singing was a natural form of expression for us both. An aria that had been rattling around in my head all that day was all that I could think of, so I began to sing it softly into the phone. *Oh, light and joy of all my heart* was the translation from Italian, which she had spoken much of her life, so I knew she would understand. Her eyes lit up as I sang, my niece told me much later. As the words began to fail me, I sang the melody only.

"You can stop now. She has gone to sleep." I heard my niece say over the phone. At that moment I knew she had slipped away while I sang to her. My sounds had opened a vibrational portal for her to pass through to her new life. Was my cousin aware of my voice over the phone? Her daughter later confirmed this. I know that when my cousin closed her eyes as if in sleep, she left her body for her next adventure in a new life. She was always adventurous.

Have you had a similar experience or something akin to it? Perhaps you desire to develop the ability you may have suspected you have to be in contact with those who have passed on.

Make an intention here.

Close your eyes

and come with me to the place

just outside of the entranceway to your mind and heart.

Let us be here a little while to consider what we are about to do.

Allow your body to be at ease.

Allow your breathing to be quiet and even.

Feel the direction of your breath as you bring it into your body—

through the nostrils, down your throat, and into your lungs.

Feel the breath as you gently breathe it out again through slightly parted lips.

For the next few breaths, be present and mindful of your breathing.

Watch any ideas or thoughts as they come in and take up space in your mind.

Just watch them as they leave without taking up residence there.

Calmly and willingly let go of them.

With the exhalation of each breath, you notice now how your body is

beginning to feel more at ease.

Your heart rate settles down. Tensions loosen.

You are coming into Quiet-mind.

Remain here during your Sounding.

Keeping your intention in mind,

bring your sounds into full voice and fill your intention

with those vibrations to bring about changes you desire.

When you come to the natural silence, remain in your Quiet-mind. Become aware of any ideas or thoughts or patterns of colors and shapes that come into your awareness. These are clues to those changes you desire.

When you are ready, inhale and exhale, open your eyes, and stretch.

Bring your outer senses back online.

You are back in your everyday world.

EXPLORATION 20:
Fear of the Body's Frailties

Your body is your vehicle for life here on Earth. Being concerned with health is a good thing. But being overly concerned with diets and weight, attempting to prevent illnesses and diseases by eating the "right" foods and taking supplements, or engaging in excessive exercise for fitness, is to court just those situations into your life by fearing them.

You are what you think! Have you heard that one before? You get what you concentrate on. Your thoughts create. What? But did we not go this round in Part 2?

It does happen that you can attract to yourself those things that you fear and dislike.

Like attracts like. By fearing a situation, you are going into the vibratory frequencies of that fear, which then becomes your reality. Remember our friend Albert Einstein's quote, "Match the frequency of the reality you desire, and that is what you get."

Enjoying being in a body is one of the main reasons for having one. If you are constantly fearful of hurting it in some way, or causing illnesses, you are truly missing the point! Using your body well, eating and drinking what you enjoy, not to harmful excess, of course, is to honor this miracle you know as your own body. Caring for it and loving it is essential for a balanced, healthy body and life.

Learn to trust that your body is capable of excellent health and wellness when you are balanced in yourself.

That is what Sounding Out Your Feelings is all about—the tool for well-being in body, mind, heart, and spirit. Use this tool to the fullest.

Fearing that your body is aging is to not recognize that each passing year you are maturing into a wonderful human being. Fear, again, begets what it fears. Enjoy each moment—each present moment—for it is all the time that you have, really.

Make your intention before we begin Sounding. Think carefully about this matter as you do.

Let us be quiet and breathe to bring your body into ease.

Feel the direction of your breath as you bring it into your body—

through the nostrils, down your throat, and into your lungs.

Feel the breath as you gently let it out again through slightly parted lips.

For the next few breaths be present, mindful of your breathing,

as you watch any ideas and thoughts coming in and taking up space in your mind.

Just watch them as they leave without taking up residence there.

Calmly and willingly let them go.

With the exhalation of each breath, you notice now how your body

is beginning to feel more at ease, your heart rate settles down,

and tensions loosen.

You are coming into Quiet-mind.

Remain here during your Sounding.

We are here at the Gateway to your mind and heart,

here to begin to find the way through that entrance.

As you continue to feel at ease, be present in the moment with your breath, paying attention to your act of breathing, while keeping yourself in Quiet-mind.

What is it that you fear regarding your health, your body, your mind?

Does your intention now reflect some of these fears that you wish to change?

Or does your intention reflect the kind of healthy body you desire to have?

With this intention in some part of your awareness,

allow your sounds to arise from deep inside you,

and let those vocal vibratory frequencies resound to your cells

and throughout your being to signify your changing attitudes.

When you come to the silence after Sounding Out Your Feelings,

remain here, still in Quiet-mind, observing any ideas, thoughts, colors, shapes, or images

that come to you. These are hints to notify you that you are in the process of changing.

When you are ready, inhale and exhale, open your eyes, and stretch.

Bring your outer senses back online.

You are back in your everyday world.

EXPLORATION 21:
"Oh, Death, where is Thy Sting?"
(Handel, *The Messiah*)

Are you afraid of the very word *death*?

There is old conditioning for humans in that word.

Let me help you uncover some of the fears attached to that word and, more specifically, the nature and workings of dying and death. Everyone must go through this process, so it may as well be now that you come face to face with some facts about it, if you haven't already. One does not have to get a terrible disease to die. Nor to suffer before dying. Those ideas, and the fears associated, are due in large part to the lack of knowledge and our cultural training around this subject.

Let us examine what happens at the exact moment of death. Although some preparatory elements may go into arriving at this moment, there is nothing mysterious, really. It is simply that the consciousness of the person leaves the body. The newly released consciousness moves on to another form of existence. Some call this state Heaven.

The body has its own form of consciousness and may take a little longer than the Spirit to release. If an illness is present in the person, then the advance of this state will run its course, and the process of dying, oftentimes, may take two or three days to arrive at its moment of release. If it is obvious that one in sickness is advancing towards death (medical staff are experienced in knowing this), the person will take what time is needed to accomplish this physical death.

However, some people have no warning of the imminent event, such as in stroke patients, or in accidents, natural disasters, or war.

Death can come at any moment in life. To be afraid of it is simply a false illusion that it can be avoided. To live the best life you can be capable of living is the best way to face the idea of dying; don't you think?

Many people fear a prolonged period of illness before death. Many problems are connected to such cases. Family is vitally important here for support of that person. If no family, or close friends, come to aid the person, then a lonely, long period may result.

There are now people who train to be end-of-life doulas who assist the dying person and help families and friends during this time.

Emotions can run high at this juncture. The person dying, the family, also the friends, all can contribute to the general atmosphere by what they bring to the event.

A doula can be of great assistance to help the family, and the patient, as they navigate through the pre-death period. Otherwise, the patient in hospital or hospice is left to the ministrations of an often-overworked staff, and may die a lonely, fearful death.

Although the medical industry is of incredible assistance in pain management and care, death is ultimately a very personal event in your life. You do it alone. Have no fear of these last moments. An understanding of the dying and death process can alleviate much of this distress.

Just try to have your life and affairs in good order, leaving little or no messes behind you for others to cope with. Early on, make a will (even if you think you have little to leave). Do you want to be buried or cremated? Make this in writing apart from your will, and include any other matters of importance to you, and make your wishes known to your family.

The moment of death is akin to going to sleep, to awaken in another realm of existence.

Nothing to fear. No hell, no damnation. Many times, the fear of this exact moment is what makes final illnesses seem so awful and drawn out.

If you have the occasion to be with a person who is ready to leave this Earth, ask if they would like you to make Sounding tones for them, if they are still capable of hearing you, or ask for the permission from those present with you. Even ask others present if they would like to join you. Explain that the sound of the human voice opens a portal of energy that the departing soul may follow, easing their way through to their next adventure. Also, the sound may be soothing to those remaining in the room. When pets leave, the same use of Sounding tones may be utilized and soothing.

Make your intention here. It can be about your own feelings on this subject.

> Let us go inward to your Inner Heart, using your breathing and
>
> sounds to uncover your own true feelings about death and dying.
>
> Close your eyes and allow your breathing to become quiet and even,
>
> and allow your body to be at ease.
>
> Feel the direction of your breath as you bring it into your body—
>
> through the nostrils, down your throat, and into your lungs.
>
> Feel your breath as you breathe it gently out again through slightly parted lips.

For the next few breaths, be present, mindful of your breathing.

Watch any ideas and thoughts as they come in and take up space in your mind.

Just watch them as they leave, without taking up residence there.

Calmly and willingly let go of them,

and with the exhalation of each breath,

you notice now how your body is beginning to feel more at ease.

Your heart rate settles down and tensions loosen.

You are coming into Quiet-mind.

Remain here during your Sounding.

Allow your sounds to rise up from within you,

and hold your intention in some part of your awareness.

Feel free to let your feelings come up to meet you. Feel grief, if you have been holding it away from you. Feel sadness, too, when it shows up, instead of forcing it down so as not to feel it. Be real with yourself, and release any emotions you fear to express regarding the mysteries around the subject of death and dying.

When you come to the silence, remain in Quiet-mind, and sit with your feelings.

Weep if you want to. Laugh at yourself if it bubbles up. Laughter can mean a release of a grief you have not been able to recognize. The death you experienced may not be of a person—it could be the loss of a career through retirement or something like this, and it can come up on you quietly a long time after the loss, and not be seen as grief for some time.

> Sound it all out, as much as you can cope with right now.
>
> When you are ready, inhale and exhale, open your eyes, and stretch.
>
> Bring your outer senses back online.
>
> You are back in your everyday world.

"There are more things in Heaven and Earth, Horatio, than are dreamt of in your philosophy."

— William Shakespeare, *Hamlet*

PART 5

EXPLORATIONS 22-30

Come with me,

And let us explore together some of those things in Heaven and Earth

which may enhance your sense of well-being in body, mind, soul and heart,

as we engage in more of Sounding Out Your Feelings,

coupled with intention and expectation,

aimed at delving into areas of self not often encountered.

So far, our journeys through the awareness of your inner and outer self have come to be a proving ground that has opened you up to new revelations of who and what you can be. These revelations have, in some ways, come through your own delving into yourself.

Through the previous Explorations, even if you skipped a few, what you have accomplished did give rise to changes in you, however big or small.

With these next Explorations, I mean for us also to look a little at your soul's growth, what that means, and how to access it.

Are you up for it? Great, if you are. I admire your courage and fortitude.

Let's have some fun exploring!

EXPLORATION 22:
What is Soul Growth?

You are Heaven on Earth as a human being.

You do not act as the animal world does. You act as a developing human, capable of reflective thinking, and of using imagination, and you have the amazing ability to be aware of past and future.

These moments of reflection set you apart as a human from the animal kingdom's ways of thinking. As you develop more of your human self, and become more aware, through developing a better knowledge and understanding of the inner workings of reality, you add to your soul's growth and development, as well as to your own human growth and development. These next Explorations may take you places yet unknown to you. These are but a glimpse into the realms of that unknown reality.

Just a suggestion, your intention here might be that as you explore further into the unknown reality, you become more aware of your soul, or spirit, and your relationship with this entity.

Let us be here a little while as we consider what it is that we are about to do.

Allow your body to be at ease.

Allow your breathing to be quiet and even.

Feel the direction of your breath as you bring it into your body—

through the nostrils, down your throat, and into your lungs.

Feel the breath as you breathe it gently out again through slightly parted lips.

For the next few breaths be present, mindful of your breathing.

Watch any ideas or thoughts coming in and taking up space in your mind.

Just watch them as they leave without taking up residence there.

Calmly and willingly let them go. With the exhalation of each breath,

you notice now how your body is beginning to feel more at ease,

your heart rate settles down, tensions loosen.

You are coming into Quiet-mind.

Remain here as you begin your Sounding.

And we are here at the entranceway to your mind, your spirit, and your heart –

and here we begin to find the way through that entrance.

Hold your intention and expectation clearly in mind,

Breathe gently and allow your sounds to arise from deep within you.

Let them soar and take you to places you had never imagined, for as long as you need.

When you come to the natural silence, remain in Quiet-mind,

and listen carefully to any words or thoughts, images, colors, or shapes that arise.

These are hints to guide you to your next experience of self. You may feel an impulse to read a certain historical book that you have recently heard about,

or you may watch something on television that catches your interest

to learn more about some spiritual material that was touched upon in that segment.

When you are ready, inhale and exhale, open your eyes, and stretch.

Bring your outer senses back online.

You are back in your everyday world.

EXPLORATION 23:
Valuing and Loving Who You Are

You do not have to be perfect to be lovable. So, cheer up!

Look at yourself differently in this moment, and discover a part of yourself that you can truly like. Yes, we have gone this way earlier. Now we deepen this search, and perhaps take a more rigorous examination. We may even discover parts of you that are not so physical, but rather spiritual or maybe just a little differently oriented.

Source, Creator, The One, God, All That Is. These are some of the names given to that infinite, loving energy that pervades all existence.

Consider this quality in the human being: the ability to love—self or others.

This ability is the reflection and expression of that overarching sense of well-being that is sometimes referred to as God's love.

Who can describe this feeling correctly, or adequately, or even find language to truly speak of this feeling? So much has been written regarding God's love. Yet that has little to do with this overall sense of Love Infinite, which is purely a feeling, not an emotion, usually meant by humans as *love*.

To come to some sense of that feeling, I suggest moving out of the head, out of the egoic ideas of the world at large, and coming down into your Heart Space, around the area of your physical heart, in the center of your chest.

Allow your attention to settle here and give permission to yourself to feel your own heart's love. If you can do this often during your day, you may feel how this center becomes more and more responsive to this feeling of love expanding here. Love grows with use. From this place, you are heart-centered in all your thoughts, feelings, and actions. Try it.

Have you found your intention for this Exploration yet?

> Come! We will go Sounding Out Your Feelings.
>
> Allow your body to be at ease.
>
> Allow your breathing to be quiet and even.
>
> Feel the direction of your breath as you bring it into your body—
>
> through the nostrils, down your throat, and into your lungs.

Feel the breath as you gently breathe it out again through slightly parted lips.

For the next few breaths, be present, mindful of your breathing.

Watch any ideas or thoughts coming in and taking up space in your mind.

Just watch them as they leave without taking up residence there.

Calmly and willingly let them go. With the exhalation of each breath you

notice now how your body is beginning to feel more at ease,

your heart rate settles down, and tensions loosen.

You are coming into Quiet-mind.

Remain here during your Sounding.

Here we are at the entranceway to your Heart Space.

Do you feel the expansion of this area near your physical heart, yet?

At first it may be a momentary sense of gentle opening,

but with some repetitions during your week,

this expansion may become a more obvious sensation for you.

Your inner heart is beginning to open to you,

showing you that you do know what love feels like.

Allow your sounds to arise from within you.

Let them soar without any effort from you,

in a joyous burst of your vocal tones, for as long as you wish.

When you come at last to the silence,

be here quietly, observing yourself.

Remain here in Quiet-mind.

Are you uplifted? Do you feel at peace?

Are you a little bit excited with this feeling?

Explore this feeling for as long as you wish.

When you are ready, inhale and exhale, open your eyes, and stretch.

Bring your outer senses back online—

taste, smell, touch, sight, hearing.

You are back in your everyday world.

EXPLORATION 24:
Your Consciousness. What is it?

What is consciousness?

You are conscious and aware. You have consciousness.

When you awaken each morning, you know yourself to be conscious, yes?

Where have you been during your sleep period? You must still have been conscious in some way, as a continuation of your waking state. You have been in the dream state. What is that? In the dream state, you experience yourself in a freer state; yet, after you wake up and remember the dream, it appears to be chaotic, fragmentary. Although, some dreams are remembered as if they were a vivid movie with you in it.

In fact, the dream world is where you may arrange to have Earthly experiences that assist you to live in a way that brings you to a more fulfilled life (if you take that road).

So, you are always aware of yourself, always conscious.

You experience your everyday awareness and

the dream state, and then there is your so-called "unconscious," that inner part of you that keeps your body moving, the blood coursing through your veins, your brain (and mind) working, your lungs breathing—you get it. You also have what is sometimes called your "super consciousness" or your higher mind. This is the hidden, and perhaps unknown, part of you, which we will tap into gently, yes, and explore what we might find there in you.

There is nothing to fear in this nonphysical realm, the metaphysical reality.

This is not the territory of outer space, where it might be possible to encounter non-humans.

I do mean the *inner you*. We will attempt to expand your conscious awareness of life and gain exciting new knowledge to help you to be more fully human than you are currently. You may even encounter yourself as yourself in other forms of reality or dimensions. This will be attempted by using intention and expectation while Sounding Out Your Feelings.

Such information regarding other dimensions may be revealed over time as you develop more of your inner abilities in these sessions, with the sounds of your own voice activating the very portions of yourself you would like to encounter. Dimensions? What are those? They are other parts of existence which operate at different, higher vibrational levels than we do on Earth.

Even your cells possess a consciousness of their own, and this is why they can react to the vibrations of your voice according to your intention for your desired outcome. Everything has consciousness and energy. In Quiet-mind you may sense a higher vibrational level than your own ordinary level, and this could be experienced as a thrill in your spine, or a tingling sensation, or any other feeling that might occur.

All of this is reflected in your Sounding voice and how you learn to respond to the vibrations of your sounds. This all may seem a bit intense, perhaps. So, we will ease gently into our Quiet-mind with your breathing. Make your intention to reflect some of your apprehensions about exploring another dimension of yourself, and to recognize which apprehensions may need to be addressed. Remember, you explore other dimensions when you go to sleep and dream.

Let us be here a while as we consider what we are about to do.

Allow your body to be at ease.

Allow your breathing to be quiet and even.

Feel the direction of your breath as you bring it into your body—

through the nostrils, down your throat, and into your lungs.

Feel the breath as you gently breathe it out again through slightly parted lips.

For the next few breaths, be present,

mindful of your breathing as you watch any ideas or thoughts

coming in and taking up space in your mind.

Just watch them as they leave without taking up residence there.

Calmly and willingly let them go.

With the exhalation of each new breath, you notice now how your body

is beginning to feel more at ease, your heart rate settles, and tensions loosen.

You are coming into Quiet-mind.

Remain here during your Sounding.

And here we are,

at the entranceway to your heart

and other layers

of existence.

Shall we go exploring?

Allow your sounds to arise joyfully from within your inner self.

Just observe and be aware of how you are reacting to your body as

you begin to see colors or shapes and notice how your emotions come up.

You may feel as if energies are circling up through you in a rush.

Breathe your way through and allow this to happen. It is like a shifting

of gears as you adjust to this new level of vibrational frequencies.

Allow your sounds to rise up within you and rejoice that you are here.

Continue Sounding Out Your Feelings for as long as you wish.

When you come to the natural silence,

be still in your Quiet-mind state,

and observe your feelings and reactions.

When you are ready, inhale and exhale, open your eyes, and stretch.

Bring your outer senses back online—

taste, smell, touch, hearing, and sight.

You are back in your everyday world.

EXPLORATION 25:
Listening to Your Environment and How it Affects You

Have you ever stopped to hear what is going on around you in your immediate environment—vehicles whizzing by, some louder than others; people talking loudly on phones or in person; aircraft flying noisily overhead; dogs barking? We live with other distracting noises, such as from construction sites, loud radios playing, and the buzzing motors of landscaping equipment. We tend to block out these seemingly endless noises from our own thoughts, if we can.

How do you react to such interference with your own sense of personal freedom to choose silence or whatever you would choose to have in your immediate environment? On an energetic level, you are bombarded by such unnatural vibratory rates. Do you feel any difference in your emotions with any one of those?

Can you tune in to your own body's reactions to those disturbing noises?

When such energy waves accost you, body, mind, and heart, they may irritate you or cause feelings of tension in the body, even as you attempt to overcome those noisy, erratic vibrations. Constant noises as in the workplace, bars, restaurants, or doctors' offices may cause disturbances in the body's own vibrational rate that result in discomfort, and perhaps, in the long run, to illness or disease.

Listening to the birds in the trees and bushes near you is such a wonderful experience. Insects and small animals can also be heard if you listen carefully. These sounds and their vibrational energies can uplift your spirits, giving you a sense of joy and wonder at Nature's gifts.

At home, are you largely free to create your own sound environment to suit your needs?

Do you love to listen to music or hear instruments being played live or people singing joyfully?

These restore your own personal energetic frequencies and help you to feel well and healthy.

Form your intention around the idea of creating your ideal environment within your own home, and furnish it, imaginatively, with those elements you would enjoy and find most suitable to your well-being in body, mind, spirit, and heart.

> Let us find a place within to encourage this environment into your reality.
>
> Allow your body to be at ease.

Allow your breathing to be quiet and even.

Feel the direction of your breath as you bring it into your body—

through the nostrils, down your throat, and into your lungs,

Feel the breath as you gently breathe it out again through slightly parted lips.

For the next few breaths, be present, mindful of your breathing as you

watch any ideas or thoughts come in and take up space in your mind.

Just watch them as they leave, without taking up residence there.

Calmly and willingly let them go.

With each exhalation of breath, notice now how your body is beginning

to feel more at ease, your heart rate settles down, and tensions loosen.

You are coming into Quiet-mind.

Remain in this state during your Sounding.

Continue your breathing pattern and,

with your intention in some part of your awareness,

let your sounds arise from within you

and soar to those vibrations of the sounds necessary

to bring you to the fulfillment of your intention.

Continue Sounding until you feel the natural silence come in.

Be still and notice what comes into your awareness.

You may at first be surprised by these images or feelings,

since they may be new to you, and difficult to figure out.

Be with these images or feelings for as long as you like.

When you are ready, inhale and exhale, open your eyes, and stretch.

Bring your outer senses back online.

You are back in your everyday world.

EXPLORATION 26:
Is it Time Now to Tap Your Emotional Reset Key?

As you have been seriously working your way through these Explorations of yourself, you have no doubt become aware of some changes in who you are, currently. Nonetheless, the problems of the outside world do take a toll on us. We need a "respite and reset" to heal and come back to well-being, and that time is NOW.

We have been particularly bombarded over these last few years by the news media and social media with horrific images of destruction by war, human outrage, ravages of our communities due to gun violence, and so much more. It is a wonder that most of us are still sane.

Those pictures are, of course, of only one probable world for us to choose to inhabit. One solution is to not turn our faces away from these horrors, but to insist on love, harmony, and peace in our own lives. We can begin, now, to bring about some kind of resolution to mankind's addiction to war, alone, or with other like-minded people, even if we don't know those people. Our hearts have been put through the wringer so often lately, that most people's nervous systems are not in good health, nor are our emotional bodies healthy.

My suggestion for an emotional and physical reset: a walk in the woods or in a garden, or singing or Sounding.

If you are fortunate enough to be able to go to a wooded area or a garden and take a walk there, stop and listen to the sounds of living things as they grow, or feel the atmosphere of the woods. Hopefully, you will be relatively alone. Breathe in this air. What do you experience?

Do you not have access to a wooded area? Then perhaps you may find a median strip between roadways where small trees or bushes grow. This area, too, has its own atmosphere, however small. Failing this, you might find a single tree growing out of the sidewalk near your home. All of these living things have consciousness and are true to their tree or plant selves.

Have you ever felt the urge to hug a tree? Here is your opportunity. Imaginatively, feel the trunk's rough surface, but also become aware of the energy flowing through that trunk. Allow your appreciation of the tree to be expressed. Be still and patient as you listen and feel the tree. Activities like these can reset your systems and adjust you to a sense of well-being, if you desire it and allow it.

Similarly, a body of water—a river, the sea, a stream, a pond—all will help to reset your systems if you take the time and opportunity to avail yourself of these wonders of nature. So much is offered to us from the natural world which we often take for granted or overlook.

Once you are back home after taking one of these excursions, either in fact or imaginatively, come and make a Sounding with your intention being something like this: "I intend that I am refreshed and reset with new vigor gained from my close association with wild, growing things in the natural world, which takes me to a better understanding of creation."

Breathe quietly and evenly,

as you allow your body to be at ease.

Feel the direction of your breath as you bring

it into your body—through the nostrils,

down your throat, and into your lungs.

Feel the breath as you gently let it out again through slightly parted lips.

For the next few breaths, be present, mindful of your breathing

as you watch any ideas or thoughts coming into your mind taking up space.

Just watch them as they leave without taking up residence there.

Calmly and willingly let them go.

With the exhalation of each breath, notice how your body is beginning

to feel more at ease, your heart rate settles down, and tensions loosen.

You are coming into Quiet-mind.

Remain here during your Sounding.

Allow your sounds to rise up from within you.

Feel the vibrations of each tone as it rides into your being,

refreshing you and bringing you into a sense of harmony.

Make your sounds until you come to the natural silence, in Quiet-mind.

Stay with these feelings, knowing that you will return to your daily life with new vigor.

When you are ready, inhale and exhale, open your eyes, and stretch.

Bring your outer senses back online.

You are back in your everyday world.

EXPLORATION 27:
"Futurizing"

When you allow yourself to often look to the future, sometimes with pleasure, at other times with a sense of dread, you are likely convinced you see a possible picture of what might happen, or of events similar to what you imagine. Yet most of these do not occur in your life at all. You may spend time worrying about what might happen based on current information available to you. You set these worries adrift in your future.

There is a frequency match with such feelings attached to old events. They have a way of popping into your reality at some future date, in some form or other. Better to stay in your present moment, where all things are possible and probable, holding to your trust that all is well now and shall be in your future, as you are intending it to be. This is a great and effective practice. You are alive and conscious here in this moment, and here are some of your treasures—your thoughts and feelings. The unfolding of the present moment creates for us the sense of time passing, and yet we are always in the spacious Present.

If it is something as "set in stone" as a medical procedure, or something of that kind, which you may be worried about, your worrying can certainly affect the outcome. Yet, most often something else will happen and you are confronted with another version of your thoughts, ideas, fears, or joys.

Similarly, looking back over your life experiences for "causes" of current problems is simply reinforcing those old events with new energy, adding to your present feelings and attitudes. Solutions may not be found there. If they are, do you see the old events in a new light and make suitable changes? Really? Think about it. Most often we tend to wallow in the emotions from past events. Not too healthy, eh? Blaming past events and those who were involved with you then, is unworthy of who you are now. You have more insight and breadth of character than to be putting the blame on another person or event, when indeed you were the original cause through your beliefs, attitudes, and feelings at those times. Everything in your environment mirrors back to you what you are. A very difficult idea to swallow, but a reality.

> Have the intention that all *is* well and *shall be* well for you.
>
> If all is well for you, then there is a fair chance it shall also be well for others,

and, if not, it is really not your business.

Just express love and well-being to them and their situations.

With this in mind, as your intention, allow your body to be at ease.

Allow your breathing to be quiet and even.

Feel the direction of your breath as you bring it into your body—

through the nostrils, down your throat, and into your lungs.

Feel the breath as you breathe it gently out again through slightly parted lips.

For the next few breaths, be present and mindful of your breathing as you

watch any ideas and thoughts coming in and taking up space in your mind.

Just watch them as they leave without taking up residence there.

Calmly and willingly let them go.

With the exhalation of each breath, notice now how your body begins

to feel more at ease, your heart rate settles down, and tensions loosen.

You are coming into Quiet-mind.

Remain in this state during your Sounding.

Keeping an awareness of your intention,

allow your sounds to arise from within you,

and let them soar, using those vibrational frequencies

to help you to achieve some of what you intend to experience.

Not everything comes to fruition as we expect.

What anxieties are you feeling now as you continue Sounding?

Are these lessening and becoming more manageable?

Let your voice resound until you know that you have come

to the natural silence, and remain in your Quiet-mind.

Sense how you feel now. What images, shapes, or colors

appear behind your eyes? Perhaps one in particular takes your interest.

Keep this image, or shape, or feeling in mind.

When you are ready, inhale and exhale, open your eyes, and stretch.

Bring your outer senses back online.

You are back in your everyday world.

EXPLORATION 28:
Mother Earth Is Sharing Her Precious Jewels with Us.

Do rocks and crystals have the power to heal? Here are some things about these treasures from Mother Earth. The subject of rocks and crystals is so often disparaged as nonsense, new-age-y, ditsy-people stuff. Yet these attitudes are not a true light to cast on this subject. Such ideas tend to dismiss out of hand the efficacy of these treasures the Earth affords us.

All life in the Universe has consciousness. Our planet is a living entity and has its own form of consciousness, just as you or I do. It is, therefore, not a great leap to recognize that anything that is taken out of the Earth has living properties, or consciousness, as well. We can say, then, that as the Earth has its own vibratory frequencies, then, so do rocks and stones, especially those that are in crystalline formations.

The crust of the Earth is mostly made up of rock, which mainly occurs in veins of quartz or quartzite. A piece of quartz stone is a powerful conductor of energy, and quartz is utilized in industry and science to harness this property. Crystalline formations are a formidable part of the world of technology, commerce, and industrial business. Some of these minerals, including thulium and cerium, are named as rare earth elements and are highly prized, especially since they are considered to actually be somewhat rare here on Earth. Rare Earth minerals are used in the manufacturing of automobiles, phones, and computers, and have many other uses in our modern world.

Can crystals be used to heal? Individual characteristic vibrations given off by each crystal, for instance, may be utilized by a practitioner who understands the various frequencies of each stone or crystal, to assist in the healing and or spiritual work this person engages in.

A person who is correctly trained in metaphysical practices and who uses some of the different vibratory emissions from powerful crystals as part of their healing services can be of great assistance to another person. Even those not trained in special work can use crystals, and, for instance, may hold them when they meditate or pray, or simply during a thoughtful, quiet period, and then may engage these vibrational frequencies of the individual crystal to enhance their intentions simply by intending to do so. This is known as programming the crystal.

Intention is thought, which creates.

Stones such as Herkimer diamonds (although not true diamonds, but double terminated quartz from Herkimer County, New York) and the beautiful flowerlike formations of Apophyllite crystals are but two of the most powerful crystals to use. Clear Quartz crystals are some of the best crystals to begin your collection. Many books are available to give more information on this subject. When looking for one to purchase, see if the crystal or stone "speaks" to you, or catches your attention in the store. Some crystals are now colored artificially. Their proper natural vibratory frequencies have been distorted by the heating process in order to color them. So be careful in your selection.

Personally, I keep a selection of stones and crystal formations both for their beauty and for their abilities to assist others and myself to support well-being in body, mind, spirit, and heart.

If you are fortunate enough to have a stone or crystal, take it up in your hand for this Sounding, and explore your experience with these energies. Sometimes it takes a little while to establish a relationship with your crystal. Be patient.

Suggestion: form your intention about your feelings regarding the use of crystals.

Keeping this intention in mind, become still,
and allow your body to be at ease.

Allow your breathing to be quiet and easy.

Feel the direction of your breath as you bring it into your body—

through the nostrils, down your throat, and into your lungs.

Feel the breath as you gently breathe it out again through slightly parted lips.

For the next few breaths, be present, mindful of your breathing

as you watch any ideas and thoughts coming in and taking up space in your mind.

Just watch them as they leave without taking up residence there.

Calmly and willingly let them go.

With the exhalation of each breath, notice now how your body

is beginning to feel more at ease, your heart rate settles down,

and tensions loosen.

You are coming into Quiet-mind.

Allow your sounds to arise from within you.

And here we are at the entranceway to your body, mind, spirit, and heart once again.

Come with me!

Looking through this entranceway, which is by now so familiar to you,

you will see from here a wonderful array of colors before you.

And on closer observation, you will see that you are looking into a garden of crystals,

some as large as you, glittering in the light, others as small as your hand,

still others so tiny you almost missed seeing them.

Many, many shapes and colors are shining in the light of the sun,

in a glorious array of stones and crystals.

Can you sense the high energies that are coming forth from these magical beings?

Are you attracted to one specific crystal? Touch it. Can you feel its energy yet?

As you begin to draw your attention away, allow your vocal tones to subside,

and come to the natural silence, and remain in Quiet-mind,

feeling the energies of the crystals. Whether you felt any energy or not, you will still receive the benefits from being with them and their vibrational frequencies.

When you are ready, inhale and exhale, open your eyes, and stretch.

Bring your outer senses back online.

You are back in your everyday world.

EXPLORATION 29:
Do I Have a Real Purpose While Here on Earth?

My cat taught me the answer to this question.

Stanley went about her business of being a cat. She knew how to live her life as a cat.

She did not stop to ask herself if she could, for instance, climb that big old tree in my backyard and climb down again. She simply did it, trusting her cat-self that she could. She did all in her life to the best of her abilities. She was good at being a cat.

My cat also knew how to love and knew she was loved in return.

As an example of this, when my husband returned home from hospital (after a little heart "oops") she leapt up onto him as he sat in his big chair, settling herself over his heart, purring.

We called her our healer cat. This was one of her many exploits in this vein. She lived her life as a true cat, being her best cat-self, whatever that was, and trusting herself.

You are a human being. Be the best human being you know how to be. Use your talents and abilities in the best way you know how. And that will be enough. Love and be loved.

Life is simpler than you think it is—this is true even on your worst days.

Intend here, perhaps, that you learn to have more trust in who you are and to live the best life you can, under even the most difficult of circumstances. Let us move now to be comfortable (and cat-like?) as we prepare to make our Sounding, with your intention in mind.

> Allow your body to be at ease,
>
> and allow your breathing to be even and quiet.
>
> Feel the direction of your breath as you bring it into your body—
>
> through the nostrils, down the throat, and into the lungs.
>
> Feel the breath as you breathe it gently out again through slightly parted lips.
>
> For the next few breaths be present, mindful of your breathing
>
> as you watch any ideas and thoughts coming in and taking up space in your mind.

Just watch them as they leave without taking up residence there.

Calmly and willingly let them go.

With the exhalation of each breath, notice now how

your body is beginning to feel more at ease,

your heart rate settles down, and tensions lessen.

You are coming into Quiet-mind.

Allow your sounds to arise from within you with the abandon of a cat.

Keep your intention in some part of your awareness.

Come with me,

to the entranceway to your mind, body, spirit, and heart.

Through those glass doors, we watch a group of kittens at play.

See how joyfully they romp while wrestling and tumbling?

They are existing in their present moment without a care,

But are being their true cat/kitten selves.

How often do you allow yourself to be just in your present moment,

without a care for the future, being your best self, right then?

When you come to the natural silence, remain here in Quiet-mind,

feeling the shifts in your energy levels

from the vibrational frequencies of your sounds.

When you are ready, inhale and exhale, open your eyes, and stretch.

Bring your outer senses back online.

You are back in your everyday world.

EXPLORATION 30:
Wherever You Go, Here You Are.

You are always here in this present moment. This moment is your point of power. It is here that you create your own reality through what you believe, through your attitudes and expectations, and through the emotions that arise from these.

> Ah, yes. Here we are again, alpha to omega.
>
> The beginning is the endpoint. So it goes, on and on.
>
> We have covered this ground much earlier in these Explorations. The cycle of life.
>
> Here is where we began our Explorations with Sounding Out Your Feelings,
>
> using your own vocal tones as your "rocket fuel" to power your intentions
>
> and expectations, to change the vibrational frequencies of your reality to that which you desired to experience.

You create your own experience of your life.

It is an awesome responsibility, having this much freedom and the free will to create.

You now know many of my secrets,

but this one is the most powerful of all.

I am confident that you have the will

and the courage to use this gift to your advantage

and to help create a better world

by being the best human you can be in this moment.

I hope that you have experienced some real changes in yourself as you explored your way through this sometimes-difficult journey.

My congratulations to you, dear friend!

You stayed the course.

Even if you skipped over one or two Explorations, perhaps their being too real or too uninteresting, you may have made changes in your attitudes and beliefs. These changes do support a more mature approach to your own life and how you continue on this new path. I trust that you shall continue on the rocky road to loving yourself in body, mind, spirit, and heart, using the gift that you give to yourself of this new tool for your self-care, Sounding Out Your Feelings.

Make those changes you want in your life.

In this moment, the only moment, the big question is: How do you feel? Feelings are anchored in our beliefs about our reality, as you now know. Ask yourself: *How have I changed by doing this work?* (The feelings file you began earlier may be helpful here).

It is my earnest hope that you are in a much better place than before we began this journey together into the heartland of your body, mind, spirit, and heart, through the use of your own vocal tones to create the vibrations of change.

Too, I hope that my sharing some of my secrets with you has been of some help to you,

and that they will continue to be of assistance in the future as you continue to use Sounding as an effective tool for your self-care. Stay in your heart center and live from here.

Continue Sounding Out Your Feelings!

ACKNOWLEDGEMENTS

My gratitude to Jane Roberts and her 'Seth Material,' and to Rick Stack for elucidating the Material for me over many years. Willard Young, voice teacher, taught me to teach others how to enhance their voices. To him my gratitude. To my long-time friend, insightful astrologer, Deborah Louth, thank you for introducing me to my editor par excellence, Lisa Tener. To Alycia Metz, gimlet-eyed proofreader, my thanks for patience beyond measure.

My husband, Charles Geard, and my children Marcus and Catherine, and their spouses Tiffany and Erik (especially Tiffany), and grandson Charlie, each deserve a medal for their loving support and technical help during this my writing adventure.

Tamara Monosoff, my publishing angel, has created an evocative and lovely cover for *Sounding Out Your Feelings*. Many thanks, Tamara.

My dear Reader, if you have gained anything of value from this book, you have my blessings for courageously attempting to do the work herein.

www.ingramcontent.com/pod-product-compliance
Lightning Source LLC
LaVergne TN
LVHW051827080426
835512LV00018B/2762